The Compassion Connection

THE COMPASSION CONNECTION

Recovering Our Original Oneness

Catherine T. Nerney, SSJ

ORBIS BOOKS
Maryknoll, New York 10545

Founded in 1970, Orbis Books endeavors to publish works that enlighten the mind, nourish the spirit, and challenge the conscience. The publishing arm of the Maryknoll Fathers and Brothers, Orbis seeks to explore the global dimensions of the Christian faith and mission, to invite dialogue with diverse cultures and religious traditions, and to serve the cause of reconciliation and peace. The books published reflect the views of their authors and do not represent the official position of the Maryknoll Society. To learn more about Maryknoll and Orbis Books, please visit our website at www.maryknollsociety.org.

Cover Art: "The Children Are Asking," copyright © Mary Southard, CSJ, www.marysouthardart.org, provided courtesy of Ministry of the Arts, http://ministryofthearts.org. All rights reserved.

The permissions listed in the Acknowledgments of this book represent an extension of this copyright page.

Manufactured in the United States of America

Library of Congress Cataloging-in-Publication Data

Nerney, Catherine T., author.
The compassion connection : recovering our original oneness / Catherine T. Nerney.
Maryknoll : Orbis Books, 2018.
LCCN 2018004170 (print) | LCCN 2018020012 (ebook) |
 ISBN 9781608337514 (e-book) | ISBN 9781626982857 (pbk.)
LCSH: Compassion—Religious aspects—Christianity. | Church—Unity.
LCC BV4647.S9 (ebook) | LCC BV4647.S9 N47 2018 (print) |
 DDC 241/.4—dc23
LC record available at https://lccn.loc.gov/2018004170

With love and gratitude for my sister, Mary Ann,
and for my brothers, Frank, John, and Tom
And for my sisters in community, the Sisters
of St. Joseph of Philadelphia

Contents

Part III
Compassion as the Spiraling Energy of the Church's Communion
How Might Our Church Resemble More Closely the Triune Heart of God?

Part IV
Compassion for the Healing of Our Aching World
Why the World Needs Us to Recover Our Original Oneness

Acknowledgments

These acknowledgments are not simply to thank people for helping me in the writing of this book. More and more, I realize the role they play in the writing of my life. The memories filling my mind and heart today overflow as deep gratitude and remind me of one of my favorite biblical passages: "The gift you have received, give as gift" (Mt 10:8, *New American Bible*, 1970). After months of preparing this manuscript, so many of those memories now wear a face of compassion or tell of its ways. Each face and every story call me to a greater responsibility to become what I remember. This is a feeble attempt to acknowledge and thank some of the many people who have come into my life and left in my heart a precious part of themselves, forging links in that compassion connection that makes us all one. Yes, you do live in me and I in you. All that I can offer you is thanks.

My first debt of gratitude is to my parents, Owen and Catherine, whose legacy of love and care for others has come to us, their children, pressed down and flowing over. Thanks for learning their lessons of self-giving love so well, Frank, John, Tom, and Mary Ann. Next, I am so overwhelmingly grateful to God for drawing me to the Sisters of St. Joseph. Little did I know at the time of entering that our mission of unioning love—"to live and work that all may be one"—would provide me with more than enough reason to get up every morning—something worth living for, even worth dying for. My life in community has been the very best gift of love incarnate for me, as we try again each morning to mirror God for one another in our many unique and quirky ways! A special "thank you" to Margaret and Ceil, Mary, Carol, and Barb, who shape our local community today and to Michelle and Kathleen, whom I still miss!

The gift of solitude and time to write were extended to me by my gracious and generous colleagues at Chestnut Hill College. I am wholeheartedly grateful to Carol Jean Vale, SSJ, PhD, our president, and our college's board of directors for granting me a sabbatical during the spring semester of 2017. My brother Tom and his wife, Christine, both of whom I love dearly, offered me beautiful space in which to pray and pace and write, while my community freed me up from all community responsibilities to do just that. So many gifts received; so many gifts to give away! Solitude provided me with the gift of presence in surprising as well as anticipated ways, as my friends companioned and supported me in this writing endeavor. For her ongoing love and friendship, I want to thank Margi Savage, SSJ, who read every word of my manuscript and so faithfully embodies what this book describes. Mary Kay, Connie, Dolores, Aida, and Phyllis, you, too, continually enrich my life, expand my heart, and encircle our world with love. Michelle and Danielle, you both hold a special place in my heart. The future grows bright, because you will help to birth a new world of compassion. It already lives in you, and there I have glimpsed its boundless contours. And then, from that great communion of saints, I draw gratefully on the compassionate presence of my dear friends Mary Scanlon, Win Grelis, and Oksana Larson. Because of them, I know firsthand that death has no power to diminish love. They live in me and I in them.

Finally, I thank Jill O'Brien, my editor at Orbis Books. Since coming on board the editorial staff of Orbis, Jill has been a trusted adviser, skilled editor, and supportive companion every step of the way. I wish her every success and great happiness in her life and profession.

I will express my gratitude to students I teach and have taught as the book unfolds, but I'll take one more opportunity here to say thanks. Teaching and learning are such mutually shared gifts; I relish more and more the privileged role that being a teacher has afforded me. To my students, thank you; thank you for sharing your lives with me inside and outside the classroom. Here's to a future full of hope: You are that hope!

Permissions

"1993. #1," from *A Timbered Choir* by Wendell Berry. Copyright © 1998 by Wendell Berry. Reprinted by Permission of Counterpoint Press.

"This Is My Song," by Susan Briehl. Copyright 2007, GIA Publications, Inc. Used by permission.

The poem "I Am Not Afraid of Death" is taken from *Threatened with Resurrection: Prayers and Poems from an Exiled Guatemalan*, by Julia Esquivel, copyright © 1982, 1994 Brethren Press, Elgin, IL. Used with permission.

"The Servant Song," by Richard Gillard. Copyright © 1977 Universal Music—Brentwood Benson Publ. (ASCAP) (adm. at CapitolCMG Publishing.com). All rights reserved. Used by permission.

"Oceans: Where Feet May Fail," by Joel Houston, Matt Crocker, Salomon Ligthelm. Copyright 2013 Hillsong Music Publishing (APRA) (adm. in US and Canada at CapitolCMG Publishing.com). All rights reserved. Used by permission.

Excerpts from *The Gift* by Daniel Ladinsky, copyright 1999, used with permission.

"The Thread," by Denise Levertov in *Poems 1960–1967*. Copyright 1966 by Denise Levertov. Reprinted by Permission of New Directions Publishing Corp.

"On the Mystery of the Incarnation," by Denise Levertov, from *A Door in the Hive.* Copyright © 1989 by Denise Levertov. Reprinted by Permission of New Directions Publishing Corp.

"The Compassion Song: Break My Heart," by Jennifer Martin. Copyright © 2001 worshiptogether.com (ASCAP) The Bridge Worx (ASCAP) (adm. at CapitolCMG Publishing.com). All rights reserved. Used by permission.

"Stranger Standing at My Door," Words: Shirley Erena Murray. 1997 Hope Publishing Company, Carol Stream, IL 60188. All rights reserved. Used by permission.

"Sanctuary," by Carrie Newcomer, found on *The Beautiful Not Yet.* Copyright © 2016. Used by permission of Carrie Newcomer.

"Pour Out Compassion and Mercy," by Briege O'Hare and Owen Smith. Copyright © 1991 St. Clare's Hermitage, Co., Kildare, Ireland. Used by permission.

"The Pool of God," by Jessica Powers, from *The Selected Poetry of Jessica Powers*, edited by Regina Siegfried and Robert Morneau. Published by ICS Publications, Washington, DC. Copyright © 1989, 1999, Carmelite Monastery, Pewaukee, WI. Used with permission.

"This Paltry Love," by Jessica Powers, from *The Selected Poetry of Jessica Powers*, edited by Regina Siegfried and Robert Morneau. Published by ICS Publications, Washington, DC. Copyright © 1989, 1999, Carmelite Monastery, Pewaukee, WI. Used with permission.

Excerpt 52 from *"Du, Nachbar, Gott . . . ,"*/"You, God, who live next door . . . ," by Rainer Maria Rilke; from *Rilke's*

Book of Hours, by Rainer Maria Rilke, translated by Anita Barrows and Joanna Macy. Translation copyright 1996 by Anita Barrows and Joanna Macy. Used by permission of Riverhead, an imprint of Penguin Publishing Group, a division of Penguin Random House LLC. All rights reserved.

Excerpt 58 from *"Ich glaube an Alles noch nie Gesagte"*/ "I believe in all that has never yet been spoken," by Rainer Maria Rilke; from *Rilke's Book of Hours*, by Rainer Maria Rilke, translated by Anita Barrows and Joanna Macy. Translation copyright 1996 by Anita Barrows and Joanna Macy. Used by permission of Riverhead, an imprint of Penguin Publishing Group, a division of Penguin Random House LLC. All rights reserved.

Excerpt 59 from *"Ich bin auf der Welt . . ."*/"I'm too alone in the world . . . ," by Rainer Maria Rilke; from *Rilke's Book of Hours*, by Rainer Maria Rilke, translated by Anita Barrows and Joanna Macy. Translation copyright 1996 by Anita Barrows and Joanna Macy. Used by permission of Riverhead, an imprint of Penguin Publishing Group, a division of Penguin Random House LLC. All rights reserved.

William Stafford, "The Way It Is," from *Ask Me: 100 Essential Poems*. Copyright 1998, 2014 by William Stafford and the Estate of William Stafford. Reprinted with the permission of The Permissions Company, Inc., on behalf of Graywolf Press, www.graywolfpress.org.

"Mother Wisdom Speaks," excerpted from *Circle of Mysteries*, by Christin Lore Weber. Published by Yes International Publishers. Used by permission.

"Come to Me," by Joe Wise © 1971, 1973, Joseph Wise. GIA Publications, Inc., publisher.

Introduction

As I begin to write, I see you, my reader, as a unique and unrepeatable face of compassion. I can say this because I choose, or rather feel compelled, not to write into a void but to picture in my mind's eye the compassionate face of each of the twenty Chestnut Hill College undergraduate students, who sat in a reconfigured circle during the past fall semester of a religious studies course titled "A God beyond All Names." And so it is for them—Masooma, Vinnie, Kadeem, Allison, the sixteen others, and the "you" I see through them—that I begin this exploration on the topic of compassion. My students will recognize it as a familiar term and one to which they had much to contribute. I hope my readers will find in it important connections as well.

I feel so privileged to be a teacher in the fields of theology and spirituality, especially as they pertain to social transformation. I often say how fortunate I am to be able to engage and speak about matters that mean so very much to me. But a deeper truth is that I get to engage and influence young people who mean even more to me than the material I teach. I trust that my own students (past and present) who read these acknowledgments will nod in agreement that they know this to be the case.

There is so much pain in our world, in our own country, our cities, our families—and in each of our hearts. We so need to find a way to help each other carry our burdens. During the months I spent in post-genocide Rwanda, I witnessed firsthand personal tragedy so immense I could hardly bear the weight of the stories the Rwandan people shared with me. And yet I stood in absolute awe of how so many of them not only survived but awoke each morning trusting that their lives held meaning and purpose beyond their grief. They were no longer victims, nor merely survivors; they were and are witnesses. As I watched them, many carrying heavy water pails on their heads and children on their backs as they trudged along, I remembered the refrain of an African song that matched their experience so well. "Our burden is heavy; we need help to bear it. Who will lift our heavy load? Who will share our sorrow?"[1] As I recalled the melody and words of the song, I heard the people themselves give answer to its poignant questions. Deep faith gave them strength to bear their heavy burdens, but it was a faith that moved them to carry each other in ways I had never imagined possible. We do live in and out of each other, I learned, as I witnessed young widows, whose own children had died violent deaths in the genocide, mothering other children who had lost their parents. They told me with utter certainty that God had preserved their lives, because these children needed them. In their own words, but even more powerfully in their actions, I saw firsthand that there is no them; there's just us. I realized how urgently we all need to live into this truth, this lost sense of our original oneness. I returned home to the United States, enlivened by the question: How can we nurture this sense of belonging to each other—this compassion connection in all of us, to help lighten the burdens we are not meant to carry alone? Our world and our very lives depend on our finding a way.

This book is the fruit of years of graduate and undergraduate teaching, keynote presentations given at both national and international conferences, seminars conducted, workshops and retreats offered, which I have reflected on

---

[1] The Iona Community in Glasgow, Scotland, sings this traditional African song, "Our Burden Is Heavy (Unzima), South Africa." It can be found on their CD, *Love and Anger*, Iona Community Wild Goose Worship Group (Chicago: GIA Publications, 2009), track 6.

and learned from—most often through the stories and comments shared by participants. But more than that intensely rich experience, the thoughts I stumble to express here and the convictions I hold most dear are the fruit of years of prayer and contemplative conversations with other spiritual seekers, close friends, and spiritual directors. In the privileged encounter of prayer, I believe that I have beheld and been held by the God of compassion who longs to be known personally, experienced intimately by each of us—without exception or reservation. The gift of this primary, divine relationship in my life, and my desire to help others to know that it is intended for them also, is what makes it possible for me to say anything at all about that which I speak. The truth I've come to know is that I don't know who I would be, or aspire to become, if this combination of prayer, reflection, and teaching did not continue to nudge me to wear a face of compassion as my own. A wise and holy Sister of St. Joseph, the congregation to which I belong, once said, "Contemplation that does not issue in compassion does not reflect the God in whose image we are created."[2] Trying to say something about this God thus seems significant; living a life of compassion is, indeed, even more so.

My primary field of study within systematic theology is ecclesiology. In studying the history and theology of the church, I have been most deeply concerned about and committed to the church's "subjective pole"—how the church's life and teaching (its objective pole) are being received by each new generation to whom they are passed on (*Dei Verbum*, 8).[3] For several decades now, I have been frustrated often and saddened greatly by my sense of a gaping disconnect between the official church's life and teaching

---

[2] Bette Moslander, CSJ, a Sister of St. Joseph from Concordia, Kansas, was a CSSJ Federation leader, esteemed mentor, and scholar on the history and spirituality of the Sisters of St. Joseph. Sister Bette died in March 2015.

[3] The Second Vatican Council's Dogmatic Constitution on Divine Revelation (1965).

and the real concerns and needs of people I meet and care about, for whom the church's life and message are intended. I write, particularly, for this group of readers, those who do not find in their experience of the church today the compassion they need to believe in themselves or in the God who desires them without condition.

I write also in support of and in gratitude for the example and leadership of Pope Francis, whose ministry over the past several years has courageously named that aching gap, pleaded for an ecclesial conversion of heart, and witnessed to a genuine church of compassion, reformed into the image of the Christ it is called to reflect and serve.

The needs of our times will not be met without a new birth of compassion, not just in our individual hearts, but in the communal heart of our church, and in other organizations and nations, who are willing to give all, to suffer and undertake all for the salvation of the outcast, the forgotten, the lost and forsaken on our roadsides, in our families, and throughout our world. We must be willing to practice compassion even while God is busy accomplishing God's transforming work in us. We must act our way into becoming the living face of God today. To be formed in the pattern of Jesus is to act more and more with his compassionate heart.

One of my personal mentors in connecting ever more indissolubly the bond between contemplation and compassion is the Trappist monk, mystic, and social reformer, Thomas Merton, who died in 1968. In Merton's prophetic/mystical work *New Seeds of Contemplation*, he speaks knowingly of the humility and courage the self-giving love of compassion requires: "To serve the God of love, one must be free, one must face the terrible responsibility of the decision to love in spite of all unworthiness—whether in oneself or in one's neighbor."[4] God's compassion knows no withholding. This

---

[4] Thomas Merton, *New Seeds of Contemplation* (New York: New Directions, 1962), 74.

God lives in all and all live in God. We belong together; we belong to one another. My personal identification with Merton's journey to radical oneness is more than a little autobiographical. Every researcher begins with a question for investigation; this question often reveals as much about the one asking it as it does about the material itself. As a Sister of St. Joseph, the vision of "living and working that all may be one" is in our DNA; it is our mission, the reason we exist.[5] Something inside me urges me to sniff out this call to unifying love wherever it can be found. In Merton the scent of the search for oneness is everywhere.

From vivid images of a confused, perceptive boyhood to the serious yearnings of a young, restless heart that would not be assuaged by the intensity of his worldly life, Merton's earliest memoirs ushered his way into a lifetime lived in "the belly of paradox," where he discovered that peace and restlessness, emptiness and fullness, solitude and communion mutually coinhere. Merton expresses something of this paradox as he concluded *The Seven Storey Mountain*, "Oh, how far have I to go to find You in Whom I have already arrived."[6] Thomas Merton's reflective life of contemplation and action found expression in the written word, particularly in his intimate journals, which today, perhaps even more than in decades past, open up such needed pathways to life in communion, where all are welcomed into God's compassionate heart, no exceptions, no exclusion. This vision of "the Oneness we already are" was given to Merton, rather than discovered by him. The gift of seeing, Merton insists, is available to us all. It is this gift of vision I pray for

---

[5] "We live and work that all may be one." This is the mission statement in its clearest and briefest form of all Sisters of St. Joseph throughout the world, who trace their origins back to Le Puy, France, in 1650. There, a group of six young French women and a Jesuit priest, Jean Pierre Medaille, received approbation for their active, apostolic work at a time when women religious were still enclosed. The rhythm of "contemplation and courageous action" has always been central to the life of every Sister of St. Joseph.

[6] Thomas Merton, *The Seven Storey Mountain* (New York: Harcourt, 1948), 419.

all who read this book and for all who share in this quest for more compassion in and for our aching world.

Many of us have pondered the powerful lines from Merton's *Conjectures of a Guilty Bystander*, where he shares his experience of standing on the busy street corner of Fourth and Walnut in downtown Louisville after seventeen years as a Trappist monk in the Abbey of Gethsemani. The mention of those seventeen years spent as a monk is by no means nonessential in Merton's compassion journey. In fact, I find it of crucial importance—the mercy of God drew Merton to the monastery, and this place served as prelude to the deep experience of oneness that he realized on a crowded street corner in the midst of an ordinary day. Return with him to that busy Kentucky intersection:

> In Louisville, at the corner of 4th and Walnut, in the center of the shopping district, I was suddenly overwhelmed with the realization that I loved all those people, that they were mine and I theirs, that we could not be alien to one another even though we were total strangers. . . . This changes nothing in the sense and value of my solitude, for it is, in fact, the function of solitude to make one realize such things with a clarity that would be impossible to one completely immersed in other cares. . . . My solitude, however, is not my own. It is because I am one with them that I owe it to them to be alone, and when I am alone, they are not "they" but my own self. There are no strangers... If only we could see each other that way all the time. . . . But this cannot be seen, only believed and "understood" by a peculiar gift."[7]

Over time, this overwhelming, unmerited gift of love and compassion transformed Merton's way of seeing all

---

[7]Thomas Merton, *Conjectures of a Guilty Bystander* (Garden City, NY: Doubleday, 1968), 156–58.

reality. By the early 1960s, a spiritually mature Merton knew by a contemplative, intuitive grasp that oneness is less a goal toward which life is pressing, as it is a return to the truth in which we have always been held. In October of 1968, just weeks before his death, Merton told a large audience of Asian monks at a Calcutta conference: "My dear brothers, we are already one. But we imagine that we are not. What we have to recover is our original unity. What we have to be is what we are."[8] A life of contemplation, awake to the Truth of who we are, has little to do with withdrawal from the world and everything to do with immersion in it through the Compassionate Heart of God, where the world is found—renewed, restored, healed, and forgiven. God's heart beats within the heart of this world. This final conviction of Thomas Merton, lover of God and God's world, grounds and directs all that follows in the next twelve chapters.

The book's claim will rest on the following four-part structure: Part I explores the character of God, first as we behold the God revealed in and through our Hebrew scriptures (chapter 1), sharing some feminine images important to uncovering compassion's depth of meaning. And then in chapter 2, we enter the Christian scriptures and behold Jesus, the visible face of our invisible God, and hear Jesus commissioning us to put on his own mind and heart by going and doing likewise (Lk 10). Part II pursues the question of how God's own heart of compassion beats in the human heart; I share some personal stories of where and in whom I have beheld the God of compassion wearing our human face(s). Chapter 3 introduces readers to my dad, offering some very ordinary but meaningful memories of how my father taught me more than I have yet fully grasped about growing into compassion as we journey home to God

---

[8]Thomas Merton, Address to International Summit of Monks, Calcutta, India, October 19–27, 1968, published in *The Asian Journals of Thomas Merton* (New York: New Directions, 1975), 51.

together. In chapter 4, you will walk with me through the hills of Rwanda and witness compassion's flow from the broken-open hearts of post-genocide Rwandan widows and others, living into the truth that there is no "them," there's just "us." The boundlessness of "the compassion connection" is seen again as chapter 5 explores the "small heart" of Etty Hillesum. In her Holocaust journals, *An Interrupted Life*, we meet this young Dutch Jewish woman whose "small heart" (her descriptor) grew so large that it reflected closely God's own heart, the One she prayed to emulate. In Part III, the church in our world today is the main focus; it is entrusted with the gift and responsibility to be the sign and the instrument of God's communion in an outpoured love, or compassion, which has no borders. Chapter 6 considers Vatican II's reclaiming of the church as a communion, whose spiraling dynamics support our growth into the likeness of our triune God—that we may be in and for the world who God is. Chapter 7 explores the vertical dimension of communion, inviting us to look up to receive communion as pure gift, for which we are totally dependent on the God who longs to give God's own self to us. Chapter 8 examines the horizontal dimension of communion, as the responsibility we share to look around and become genuine communities in which we take care of each other, where compassion is lived out in lives handed over into each other's keeping. Chapter 9 challenges readers not to be content with the building up of loving communities here and now, because the eschatological or universal dimension of communion thrusts us beyond ourselves into a future that is not yet, where God's reign comes as unbounded compassion—all alive in God and God alive in all, perfectly One. As we give ourselves over to this work of God in and for the world, chapter 10 offers the final dimension of communion as the kenotic invitation to become a poorer, humbler church, one willing to grow a bit smaller, even die to what we thought ourselves to be, so that the inexhaustible Mystery of Compassion may become all in all. Part IV focuses on compassion as the energy needed to heal our aching world. Chapter 11 invites each of us to become the change we hope to see in the world by our efforts to embody communion in our person-to-person, group-to-group communication. The chapter examines the much-needed skills of listening and speaking from the heart. Finally, in chapter 12, we listen again to the echo coming loudly from God's own heart of compassion, pleading with us to take care of each other, for God's sake. This final chapter looks at one concrete situation in our world today—the global migration crisis—and asks how the migration of so many millions of our sisters and brothers around our world challenges us to live into the truth that we are one human family, sharing a compassion connection that must prove stronger than any attempt to divide us into them and us. We are in need of reshaping the entire human landscape; our very lives may depend on how we give ourselves to, and receive the lives of, those who seek refuge among us. We have been made for these times, when the very future of the human family and life on our planet is counting on our becoming a fuller version of our human/divine selves. Will we live what we have beheld?

The Compassion Connection: Recovering Our Original Oneness is one small attempt to help awaken us to the truth of who we are and the connections that bind us together as one in this world that God so loves. As you begin to read the following chapters, I invite you to get in touch with a primary question to guide you. The truth is that I, as author, consider the material you will read here secondary to you, the reader. Your own unique life serves as the primary text you will explore in these pages. If you do not discover something more about yourself, about your relationship with God, and all others, in this reading, I will not have achieved one of my primary goals in writing the book. For this self-discovery to happen, you must be willing to read reflectively, to test what you read in the context of your own experience, and to pay attention to pulls and nudges deep within, inviting you to see and become more of yourself, as a unique and unrepeatable face of compassion, despite what you might need to give up in the process. It's my hope that, like Thomas Merton, we may find ourselves in "the belly of paradox" where each fall will teach us more about rising, each loss more about finding, each giving over more about receiving, and each death more about living into the Holy Mystery of the Compassion Connection. Remembering who we are enables us to love and be loved, without barriers or fear. In this God who holds us all, we stumble into the powerful truth of our original oneness.

PART I

COMPASSION
AS THE CHARACTER
OF GOD

*Who Is This God Who Wants
to Be Known by Us?*

1

Behold Your God

Encountering God in Our Hebrew Scriptures

Check in with Your Own Experience

Years ago I was caught by the words of a song by Joe Wise, titled "Come to Me." The refrain stays with me and repeats itself somewhere in my heart: "Come to Me and I will give you Me and I'll give you back to you. Behold I make all things new for you, with you, in you. Come to Me and I will give you Me and I'll give you back to you."[1] I've come to believe these words; in fact, I count on them. God does long to give Godself to me and to give me back a truer version of me—one that resembles the God whom I behold a little more closely. If we are, indeed, created in the image of some God, then our primary task as humans is to discover something about this God, in whose image we have been made, in whose likeness we are called to grow. The great biblical scholar Walter Brueggemann spoke compellingly about this theological task: "We will not have a politics of justice and compassion unless we have a religion of God's freedom. We are indeed made in the image of some God. And perhaps we have no more important theological investigation than to

---

[1] Joe Wise, *A New Day* (Chicago: GIA Publications, 1973).

discern in whose image we have been made."[2] Who among us does not want to figure out who we are supposed to become? Let's suppose that this self-discovery depends less on our "figuring out" and more on our opening up to receive the self who will be revealed as a unique reflection of the God who wants to be seen and known by us.

It is my great hope, as you begin to read this book on compassion, that you'll test everything you read against the backdrop of your own experience, past and present. Enter into a time of prayer. Don't be frightened away. Rather, please hear this as a caring request that you take some personal time alone with the Alone, even if it interrupts your reading, to let yourself be held. It does not matter all that much if God, as Compassion, has been revealed to others, if you can make no connection at all with such a God in your own personal life. I have a hunch that far too many people give up on a need for or a desire to encounter God because the image of God they've been offered is either judgmental and frightening or simply distant and uninterested. On the contrary, the God who longs to come to you, who is waiting to be held by you, is incredibly close, waiting for you to open yourself to see that this God already dwells within you and loves you immensely.

One memory that rushes back to me as I issue this invitation is a comment of a student just last semester. After asking students to consider if they have met this unconditionally loving God anywhere in their experience of life thus far, Daphney responded that she never encountered this God that I describe, but she has come to believe that this could happen for her and she looks forward to it. Well, that's a place to start—just such willingness. Yes, God asks for nothing more from any of us. God is much more intent and ready to make this meeting take place than I am able to make it happen, though I feel so eager to help others discover this

---

[2]Walter Brueggemann, *The Prophetic Imagination* (Philadelphia: Fortress Press, 1978), 17.

incredible Lover of us all. So what does such an encounter ask of us, where do we look for God to show up?

The risk I invite you to take now is to journey inside to have a deeper look. Perhaps this invitation to "Behold your God" will require some clearing out. That's regularly what I need to do. How do I keep accumulating so much clutter, so many distractions and concerns, which block my capacity to behold the God who beholds me with so much love, a love I name compassion? But in naming that love I'm jumping ahead of myself a bit. The truth is I have come to claim my experience of being loved by God first, before ever doing anything to merit such undivided, untiring attention, because others before me have had similar experiences and they have helped me understand and validate my own. Thomas Merton names this disposition of knowing oneself to be already loved and accepted as faith. He explains it this way: "The root of Christian love is not the will to love, but the faith that one is loved. The faith that one is loved by God—loved by God though unworthy—or rather irrespective of one's worth."[3] It's all gift; we simply open to receive it!

This work of clearing out, opening up inner space for the divine coming, asks only for some silence, some stillness—some room. Prayer simply asks us to make ourselves available. The invitation to gaze and listen can help frame a prelude to God's approach—the divine/human encounter of contemplation. Pay attention in the quiet to where a bush catches fire in you (see Exodus 3). It may be the face of someone you love, a glance at nature, a line from a poem or song, a passage from scripture, a favorite prayer, or a kind word someone recently spoke to you that comes back to your mind's eye. By contrast, it might be a struggle you're facing, a loss you're experiencing, a concern that weighs on you. Hold these gently as well. Let these thoughts or images catch your attention in the quiet. This may be God

---

[3]Thomas Merton, *New Seeds of Contemplation* (New York: New Directions, 1961), 73.

trying to say more to you. At least I've come to trust these inner drawings. They are readily available to all of us, if we will only pay attention. As you focus on the one that keeps coming back, trust that you are not doing this attending alone. Behold God beholding you with love, as you hand over this thought, image, concern to your God, or listen as God expresses a desire to carry it with you.

Since as long as I can remember I have come to identify God's approach with a certain lump in my throat which wells up, usually totally unexpected, when something fills me with wonder or awe, with appreciation or inspiration, with yearning or a sense of my own unworthiness. These emotions may seem abstract, but the swelling within me is very real and concrete. I've tried to explain this feeling of being ready to burst with a sense that God just seems bigger than I can contain, which of course I cannot. One of my earliest memories of trying to control this inner surge happened when I was in eighth grade. It was a Tuesday evening in early spring and the eighth-grade girls were being inducted into the parish Sodality of Mary. For me as well as most of my friends this meant being able to meet each other on a school night, when ordinarily we would not be able to go out. We waited on street corners as the group arrived, about eight of us, to walk down to church together and catch up after not having seen each other for about three hours. After the ceremony was over, we'd have a chance again to walk each other home, be together and talk some more. The funny thing that happened, however, was that something genuinely moved me as the prayer was ending that evening. Lights went out in the dark church and with only candles to cast the glow, we stood to sing a song to Mary. That's when it happened—the lump in my throat. There was more going on here than the chance to be with my friends on a school night. It would be impossible for me to count all the times that lump has recurred in my experiences of ordinary moments that overtake me with a goodness bigger than me. I've come to trust them. I can even ask important questions about their meaning and what I am meant to do with them. But it was a graduate student, Peggy, who helped me with this piece of welcoming God's approach.

During a graduate spirituality course on conversion and grace, Peggy shared an experience she had had as a sixth-grade teacher. A substitute had taken her class for two days while Peggy attended a conference. At the conclusion of that second day, the substitute teacher reported to her an incident that occurred in the schoolyard that afternoon, where several of Peggy's students were involved in a fight. The sub had handled it but felt that Peggy ought to know. When Peggy returned the next day, she spoke with her class about her feelings on learning what had happened in her absence. And she wanted to listen to them describe the unfortunate event. One by one, students spoke honestly and repentantly about their wrongdoing. Peggy recounted that as she listened, something very unusual happened. She felt herself fill up as a lump in her throat took her completely off guard. "I rarely cry," Peggy admitted, "but I realized in an overwhelming way how much I love these kids; I felt such pain that they could actually hurt each other. I whispered to myself right then and there: 'Is that You, God, welling up in me with love for your children?'" I love Peggy and her story. I love her question particularly. I find myself repeating it quite often when that lump appears. "Is that You, God?" I just want to pay attention when God is trying to break through. Do you have any signs you can identify with the too-much-to-hold character of God?

Meeting the God of Our Hebrew Scriptures

So much can be learned by reflecting on how these God-sightings happened for our ancient Hebrew ancestor in faith, Moses. A shepherd and sojourner in Egypt, he was just trying to be faithful to his daily life of tending the flock of his father-in-law, Jethro. A piece of Moses's story, as recounted in the Book of Exodus, leads us directly to the kind of God revealed to him and to us. The text of our Hebrew scriptures clearly emphasizes that God is not interested in being boxed up in a static name—God is no-name, the un-nameable YHWH. God wants to share with us the divine nature—God's character—God's way of being God. On Mount Horeb, Moses beheld a bush burning without being consumed and heard a voice say: "I have beheld the suffering of My people and have come down to set them free" (Ex 3:7). God promises at Horeb to be with Moses as he leads his people. From Mount Horeb to Mount Sinai, God walks with Moses and again reveals more of God's character. In Exodus 34, we hear God's manifesto, which has become a kind of credo or belief statement, about who God is and how God longs to be known by each of us, his beloved children. In Exodus 34:6, God proclaims that God is compassionate and gracious, slow to anger and abounding in steadfast love. These attributes of God need pondering.

Pondering the Divine Character and Some Implications

According to God's own self-revelation, "God is *rechem/rachamin* (Hebrew), meaning compassion, mercy, lovingkindness."[4] Translations of the Hebrew most carefully connect *rechem* with the feminine for womb. God's way of being poured out in the world is womb-love. That *rechem* kind of love is further described in Greek as *splanknizoi-mai*—literally the internal organs of the mother's womb—there can be no missing this meaning.[5] Quite honestly, I find

---

[4]Geiko Müller-Fahrenholz, "Turn to the God of Mercy: New Perspectives on Reconciliation and Forgiveness," *Ecumenical Review* 50, no. 2 (1998): 196ff.

[5]Walter Kasper, *Mercy: The Essence of the Gospel and the Key to Christian Life* (Mahwah, NJ: Paulist Press, 2013), 42. "It is characteristic of the Old Testament that it uses the expression *rachamin* for compassion and also for mercy. This word is derived from *rechem*, which means womb; the term can also refer to human intestines." Pope Francis explains the Greek word *splanchnizoimai* as compassion and also as "the word that indicates internal organs of the mother's womb. . . . It is a visceral love. God loves us in this way with compassion and mercy." *Pope*

this mind-blowing and heart-rending! I'd like to suggest that the rest of this book will be an effort to help unpack some of the implications of experiencing God as womb-love—implications for how we are to live as persons, as a church, and as a world, hearts wherein God can recognize God's own becoming.

Because this opening chapter has invited you to behold God in prayer, it might be fitting to suggest one meaning of compassion or womb-love to keep in mind. A womb provides a safe, holding place for life to grow. Let this space, which God provides for all, become in you a sacred spot, an expansive opening in your own heart, where God and you can indwell—you in God and God in you. As a child lives within her mother, and the mother gives over her very life blood for her child, so the God of life, Compassion itself, gives life to our world. If you return to this sacred space within—Just let it find you!—you will discover quite simply and profoundly that compassion is God. From that place in you, everything you look out on changes. You begin to see that compassion gene in everyone, birthed from and sustained in that same womb of Love. "I live in me and in You."[6] Steeped in the wisdom and witness of the great, Hebrew prophets, Rabbi Abraham Joshua Heschel saw it for himself: This encounter is intended for us all, no exceptions. It is who God is.

The Compassion of God in the Psalms and Prophets

It seems important to offer at least a few examples of how this credo of God's character brought the Hebrew people back to their faith each time they were tempted to choose another kind of powerful, angry God to claim as theirs. Some of the most poignant images of God's untiring love and faithfulness are captured in the words of the prophets.

Francis: The Name of God Is Mercy (New York: Random House, 2016), 129.

[6]Abraham Joshua Heschel, "I and You," in *The Ineffable Name of God: Man* (New York: Continuum, 2007), 31.

In Hosea 11, the prophet has God speak to God's unfaithful people, who insist on turning away. "How can I give you up, O Ephraim? How can I hand you over, O Israel? . . . My heart recoils within me, my compassion grows warm and tender." Instead of the people being cast aside for their evil ways, the subversion takes place in God's own heart. God's compassion flares up, and God decides not to execute his burning wrath. Mercy is victorious over justice in God. Mercy doesn't trump justice; it transcends it. Mercy is the profound mystery of who God is. "For I am God and no mortal, the Holy One in your midst and I will not come in wrath" (Hos 11:9). The fundamental characteristic of God, elevating the divine above all humans, is God's boundless mercy, God's womb-like love. With gratitude and awe for such a God, the psalmist prays: "For you, O God, are good and forgiving, abounding in merciful love to all who call on you" (Ps 86:5) and again in Psalm 103:1—"As a father has compassion for his children, so the Lord has compassion for all who fear Him." And: "The Lord is compassionate and gracious, slow to anger and abounding in merciful love" (Ps 103:8; 145:8).

Yet this God of limitless compassion was for the Israelites of old, as such a God is for us today, often more than they could take. Too much compassion and forgiveness, too many unrelenting second chances are embarrassing! Who can put up with such a God, let alone aspire to grow into such behavior? The Book of Jonah, a wild tale of our human incomprehension, may provide the very best example of our dilemma. Faced with a God who turns God's own heart inside out and has compassion on sinful Nineveh, after Jonah had threatened its destruction, what is Jonah to do? He runs away. It's such a timeless story of all of us, confronted by a God who loves so tirelessly, that Thomas Merton ends his book *The Sign of Jonas* by having God ask this question: "Have you not seen me, Jonah, my child? Mercy within mercy within mercy. I have always overshadowed Jonah with my Mercy and cruelty I know not at all."[7]

God's relentless care for those who are poor and suffering is the visible expression of our compassionate God, which moved the prophets from the praying stance of the psalms to courageous action on behalf of God's children in need (Amos, Hosea, Ezekiel, Jeremiah, Baruch, and Zechariah, to name just a few). That God's very life imprints in us that same dynamic rhythm from prayer to action, from contemplation to lives of compassion, reveals the God in whose image we are made.

Resembling the One Who Births Us

Throughout salvation history, those who have encountered this living God extend to us the same message, filled with the same awareness—to become who we are. The thirteenth-century mystic, Mechthild of Magdeburg, hears God put it this way: "Pour out compassion and mercy from the depths of your heart. Then you will resemble Me, Your God, and I will make you whole."[8] In this context, the wholeness we all seek means our becoming another face of God, like the One who birthed us all. How do you or I resemble God? It might be helpful to ask someone who knows us well to count the ways. There are times when I don't think I'm up for their possible answer, but the presence in my life of those who know me best, and love me still, calls me to want to be better.

That thought of growing more like the one who gave us life in the first place reminds me of an experience I had with my own mother several years back. As I prepared to leave the doctor's office with her one late summer afternoon, the doctor himself came out, ready to go home for the day. He

---

[7]Thomas Merton, *The Sign of Jonah* (Orlando, FL: Harcourt, 1953), 362.

[8]Briege O'Hare, "Pour Out Compassion and Mercy," on *Woman's Song of God: Songs Inspired by the Writings of Women Mystics* (Hermitage Productions, 2011), track 6. Based on Mechthild of Magdeburg, *Flowing Light of the Godhead*.

walked across the room, shook my hand, and spoke to my mother. "Catherine, you'll never be dead as long as she's alive." His words to her stay with me still. Of course, the doctor was referring to my close, physical resemblance to my mother. I had heard that often before and since, but there was something more I was hearing on this summer afternoon that gave me pause to ponder: "What is it to recognize myself in another and another in me?" The doctor was, no doubt, making a passing comment. For me it expressed a significant claim. I, who once found life within my mother, was in turn responsible for my mother's ongoing life in me. The mother/child relation was somehow mine to continue. The Buddhist monk Thich Nhat Hanh tells a beautiful story about an experience he had following his mother's death which makes this point very powerfully:

> The day my mother died I wrote in my journal, "A serious misfortune in my life has arrived." I suffered for more than one year after the passing away of my mother. But one night in the highlands of Viet Nam, I was sleeping in the hut of my hermitage. I dreamed of my mother. I saw myself sitting with her, and we were having a wonderful talk. She looked young and beautiful, her hair flowing down. It was so pleasant to sit there and talk with her as if she had never died. When I woke up it was about two in the morning, and I felt very strongly that I had never lost my mother. The impression that my mother was still with me was very clear. I understood then that the idea of having lost my mother was just an idea. It was obvious in that moment that my mother is always alive in me.[9]

This kind of mutual interdependence I sense to be true. We live in and through one another. We become ourselves only

---

[9]Thich Nhat Hanh, *No Death: No Fear: Comforting Wisdom for Life* (New York: Riverhead Books, 2002), 5.

in and through a process of mutual inter-becoming. It all began in God's own creative, self-giving love. Much deeper than the inevitability of my resembling my earthly mother is the reality of my core identity, the core identity of all who bear the same family resemblance, a unique but related face of compassion—the same Divine Love has birthed us all. God will never be dead as long as we're alive.

Growing more like the Divine Lover in whose image we are created doesn't happen overnight or without its ups and downs. At times I forget that Self-giving Love that has given me life. At other times, I resist it, because the cost of becoming compassion—of giving myself away in love—is just too risky and I'm afraid of losing myself in the process. What fills me with hope and courage is the faith that reminds me over and over again, especially when I am most resistant or forgetful, that God is greater and more loving than all my selfishness and human fears. I trust that in the end God's outpoured love will prove stronger than any of my counter-pulls to get away. I'm counting on that not just for me but for all of us.

A powerful, true story written by Nicholas Gage illustrates something of this compassion connection for me. In 1948, at the age of nine, Nicholas had escaped from Greece along with his three sisters during Greece's civil war to join his father, who had lived in the United States since World War II. His mother, Eleni, had been captured by the communist guerrillas for trying to save her children by getting them out of the country safely. Eleni was tortured and killed, while Nicholas grew up in Massachusetts with deep and painful memories of his mother and her sacrificial love for her children. Nicholas Gage went on to become a prominent *New York Times* journalist. He spent much of his time and talent researching and writing about the events of his mother's life beyond the fragmented memories of a nine-year-old child. Gage interviewed hundreds of people who knew Eleni, as well as communist guerrillas responsible for terrible atrocities, who were now thought of as heroes in the sixties and seventies of post–civil war Greece.

By 1981, Nicholas Gage had left the *Times* and moved his family to Greece, resolving to find his mother's killer. In the summer of 1982, with a gun in his back pocket, Nicholas climbed the stairs to the apartment where he knew his mother's killer, a man named Katis, was spending the afternoon alone, while his family was at the beach. He found the old, frail Katis asleep on a chair. He didn't even need his gun; a pillow pressed over the old man's gaping mouth would work just fine. Gage ends his biography with a final account of how his life's work—to avenge his mother's death—turned out:

> I stood staring at the man who had killed my mother for a few minutes, perhaps more. Then I turned around and walked out, closing the door softly behind me. I had found the perfect opportunity for killing him and I couldn't do it. At the end of my long journey I learned that I didn't have the will. . . . During my long search, I learned much about my mother's nature . . . not to join in hating, but in loving. . . . If I killed Katis, I would have to uproot that love in myself and become like him, purging myself as he did of all humanity and compassion. . . . My mother's love, the primary impulse of her life still binds us together, often surrounding me like a tangible presence. Summoning the hate necessary to kill Katis would sever that bridge connecting us and destroy the part of me that is most like Eleni.[10]

This wasn't the ending the gifted author, Nicholas Gage, or the wronged son, expected to write. He had the perfect opportunity, but he "didn't have the will." Could it be that there is Something bigger inside us, urging us to become our best human selves, even when inhumanity threatens the best in us? Is there simply no limit to God's sustaining power of love to prevail over the most evil and hateful human impulses? Nicholas Gage witnesses to the unfath-

---

[10]Nicholas Gage, *Eleni* (New York: Ballantine Books, 1982), 469–70.

omable strength of this bond. His mother lives on in him. This indwelling of love, which is our true identity, shows up in less dramatic ways as well. I bet you have examples of your own. The love of someone brings out the best in you.

Here's another example of a God who won't be dead as long as we're alive! Paul Coutinho recounts this story in his great little book, *How Big Is Your God?* It is a simple story my students always remember and have retold often. It describes a grandmother who goes Christmas shopping with her young grandson and, while choosing gifts for him, she notices a little girl, obviously poor and alone, peering through the store window. She goes out and invites the child to come in and choose a gift for herself. After selecting a big, stuffed animal, which she hugs closely to her little body, she looks up at the boy's grandmother and asks in great wonder: "Are you God? "No," comes the immediate answer. "But," said the woman, "I am a child of God." "Oh," the little girl said with great delight, "I knew there was a connection."[11] Yep. Here's the compassion connection. This little girl belonged to the grandmother, just as her biological grandson did. That's some lesson for this young boy to learn from the big, compassionate heart of his grandmother. There is no them; there's just us. As God's children, we belong to each other. Hmmm . . . what do you think?

I often return to a poem of Denise Levertov to affirm my faith that the thread binding me with God and others has not been and cannot be severed:

> The Thread
> Something is very gently,
> invisibly, silently,
> pulling at me—a thread
> or net of threads
> finer than cobweb and as

---

[11]Paul Coutinho, *How Big Is Your God? The Freedom to Experience the Divine* (Chicago: Loyola Press, 2007), 1.

elastic. I haven't tried
the strength of it. No barbed hook
pierced and tore me. Was it
not long ago this thread
began to draw me? Or
way back?

Was I
born with its knot about my
neck, a bridle? Not fear
but a stirring
of wonder makes me
catch my breath when I feel
the tug of it when I thought
it had loosened itself and gone.[12]

Have you felt the wonder and the tug of it? Have you felt that pull toward love nagging you to give yourself to others, reminding you that it is your true nature? Loving selflessly becomes you!

Conversation Starters

1. *Are there distractions that clutter your inner space and create obstacles to silence and stillness in your life? How does our culture make it difficult to find space to do this inner work?*
2. *What other implications can you find in thinking of God as womb-love? What difference does this meaning hold for how we see others, especially those outside our immediate family of origin? Given this understanding, what do you see as the opposite of compassion, the opposite of God?*

---

[12]Denise Levertov, "The Thread," in *Poems, 1960–1967* (New York: New Directions, 1983), 50.

2

Behold Jesus

The Visible Face of Our Invisible God
in Our Christian Scriptures

The God of Compassion Wears
Our Human Face in Jesus

As God's children, all birthed from the same Divine Womb of Love, we belong to one another. At some deep level, many of us believe this; but for me, at least, it helps to admit that seeing helps believing. How wonderful that from time to time, we catch a glimpse of what this looks like in someone who seems to love everyone without borders, beyond the ties of family and a close circle of friends. Is this really what it looks like to image God's compassion?

Our Jewish sisters and brothers provide witness of what it means to rely on the biblical word of the Hebrew prophets to compel them to live compassion in action. Along with them, we as Christians deepen our faith vision of God, the Compassionate One, through attending to the voice of the prophets and praying the psalms. Take care of the widow and the orphan, the prophets remind us (see Is 58).

As Christians, we believe that our preeminent source of empowerment meets us in the Person of Jesus of Nazareth, a prophet and more than a prophet. The writer of John's gospel makes this clear; we have seen and can testify that compassion took on our human flesh and has walked our life journey all the way through death to new, risen life—life for all. God's invisible life as compassion has been made visible in Jesus, God's own compassion in human flesh and history. In the profound Mystery of the Incarnation, we have God with us in our human likeness. What does compassion look like, we have every reason to ask, when we see far too often what it is not? Compassion looks like Jesus. Behold Jesus and learn from him (Mt 11:28). Listen and hear Jesus say to you: "Come to Me and I will give you Me, and I'll give you back to you" (Joe Wise). The revelation is astounding—as many teachers in the early centuries of the church proclaimed, "God became human so that humans could become divine."[1] This conviction, known as *theosis,* or deification, has never been lost in the Eastern church. Humanity is meant to grow into divinity. In the West, we have too often feared this outlandish claim and tried to diminish it with an emphasis on human sinfulness. But the two claims of our creaturehood do not need to exclude each other. God loves us in our very sinfulness and has saved us for our birthright—participation in God's own life. There is a lovely line from the fourteenth-century Sufi mystic Hafiz that echoes a similar refrain: "Love, so God will think 'Ahh-hhhh, I've got kin in that body.' "[2] That God may recognize God's very life growing in us! We see what God looks like in the life of Jesus, in whom God took great delight. Yes, here is God's kin, we hear at the time of Jesus's baptism when a Voice from heaven declared: "This is my Beloved Son in whom I am well pleased" (Mt 3:17; Lk 3:21).

Throughout the gospels, we meet Jesus on his daily

---

[1] Some have attributed this claim to St. Athanasius (296–373) from his *On the Incarnation,* but most patristic scholars agree that this idea was so prevalent in the early church, in the writings of Irenaeus, Justin Martyr, and Clement of Alexandria before Athanasius, that it is difficult to be certain of its original source.

[2] Hafiz, "I Got Kin," in *The Gift: Poems by Hafiz, the Great Sufi Master*, trans. Daniel Ladinsky (New York: Penguin Compass, 1999), 330.

rounds, making his way through the cities and towns of Palestine, climbing hills and walking seashores, an itinerant teacher and healer of every ill. Wherever Jesus went, crowds flocked to him, because in him, people found unconditional acceptance, infinite respect, and life-giving direction. They came to believe in themselves, to care for one another, and to trust in the loving reign of God both within and beyond them. Just to touch the hem of his garment brought healing, peace, and freedom (see Mt 9:18–22). What made the presence and touch of Jesus so appealing, even transformative? He did so much more than bring the message of a compassionate and all-merciful God; he *was* the message. In the fourth chapter of the gospel of Luke, we read that on entering the synagogue of Nazareth, Jesus was handed the sacred scroll, which he opened to the Prophet Isaiah. On finishing the reading of the text, Jesus declared that that day the prophecy of Isaiah was fulfilled in their hearing. Jesus himself brought "release to the captives, sight to blind eyes and liberation to those oppressed" (Lk 4:16–19, 21). This is what compassion looks like. To be about this work in the world is to be God's own reflection, and Jesus shows us the way. Over and over again throughout the gospels, Jesus reaches out to touch those hurting with hands of healing, with a heart of forgiveness, with acts of compassion, that welcome all and refuse to exclude anyone from love's embrace. All Jesus asks from each of us is a willingness to open ourselves to life, to expand our circle of care, to believe that we can make a difference in our world. Do we really try to live into this bigger sense of ourselves—who we are and who we can become? Can we remind each other by how we live today?

The *Rechem* Heart of Jesus

If the multiple gospel examples of Jesus as the face of compassion incarnate are not enough evidence of the link between the credo of the Hebrew understanding of God and the life of Jesus, there's more to be said about the direct connection the gospel writers intended. The Hebrew scriptures reveal to us not a name for God, but the very character of the Divine, as we've already seen. God is self-giving, outpoured love, identified with *rechem*, womb-love. Such selfless, unconditional, limitless love appears again, using the same Hebrew word, *rechem*, to describe the heart of Jesus in the gospels.

Here in the United States, where Valentine's Day celebrations feature hearts of endless variety, it hardly feels necessary to say anything further about the use of the word "heart" as symbol, rather than a physical organ. That we have come to identify the heart with love, as so many emojis remind us, is not news. But how we use the word "love" to mean so many feelings and actions suggests a need to greater refine the symbol of the human heart and the authentic meaning of love. The word "heart" will be used frequently in this text; each time, I intend something akin to this authentic meaning. As a symbol, the heart both points to and expresses the core identity, the center of value and purpose for each one's unique life. I'd like to add to our understanding of "heart" a theological reflection to underscore the significance of referring to the Sacred Heart of Jesus, the center of his identity, as well as ours. As the great theologian Karl Rahner points out, to speak of the heart of Jesus, for the Christian, is to refer to God's own heart.

> The center of our hearts has to be God; the heart of the world has to be the heart of our hearts. God must send us God's heart so that our hearts can be at rest. . . . And God has done it. And the name of God's heart is Jesus Christ. It is a finite heart and yet it is the heart of God. When it loves us then we know that the love of such a heart is only love and nothing else. . . . In the heart of Christ our heart knows that it is one with the heart of God. It knows it is one with the heart of God,

in which even the thief and the murderer find pardon, one with the heart in which our darkest nights are transformed into days, because Jesus has endured the nights with us. It knows that it is one with the heart in which everything is transformed into the one love.[3]

The gospel writers, centuries earlier, used the same word to describe Jesus's heart that the Hebrew scriptures use to describe the character of God. Jesus's heart is *rechem*. You may be familiar with gospel passages that talk about the heart of Jesus being "moved with pity," an alternative English translation of *rechem*—the poured-out, self-giving love that is God. Take for example the scene in both the gospels of Matthew and Mark where Jesus sees the crowds gathered around him and his heart is moved with pity because they are harassed and helpless, like sheep without a shepherd (Mt 9:36; Mk 6:34), and similarly Jesus's heart is moved by pity when the crowds spend days in a deserted place listening to his words and are hungry. Jesus will not send them away without giving them something to eat (Mt 15:32; Mk 8:2). Jesus's heart is revealed as compassion, poured out in love for those in need, all loved by him and by God. While passing through the city of Naim, Jesus sees a widow weeping, as her only son is being carried out for burial. "Moved with pity," Jesus touches the corpse, raises the young man from the dead and gives him back to his grieving mother (Lk 7:11–15).

Growing into a Heart like Jesus

The heart of Jesus is the heart of God here with us in human flesh. If our hearts are to resemble God's heart, as seen in the heart of Jesus, love takes on a peculiar, precise

---

[3]Karl Rahner, "The Mystery of the Heart," in *The Great Church Year: The Best of Karl Rahner's Homilies, Sermons and Meditations* (New York: Crossroad, 1994), 243.

way of being in the world. Our hearts resemble the heart of God when they, too, are poured out in self-giving love for all without exception. If in God's heart, both thieves and murderers find forgiveness, where does this kind of loving show up outside the heart of Jesus? Is such selfless, mother-like love possible? Has anyone else put on this heart of God in human flesh? Only the gospel of Luke uses the word *rechem* to describe any heart other than Jesus's and that occurs twice in Luke's gospel.

Try to enter the following gospel stories, whether or not they are familiar to you. Perhaps, if they are not, they may have more significance, heard for the first time. If you've heard them repeatedly, let them fall on your heart afresh now—let your heart open to listen attentively for something new or unexpected. The first story I want to share appears in the fifteenth chapter of Luke's gospel. Jesus uses several different analogies to show how God seeks out those who are lost, who feel in any way unsafe, unwanted, or disposable. Jesus begins with the story of a lost sheep, moves on to talk about a lost coin, and finally, he tells of a lost son. Jesus longs to have his hearers understand how much God desires that no one be lost or forgotten. God reaches out to bring all into the unconditional loving space of God's own heart. As Jesus, the storyteller, proceeds, we meet a father of two sons, the younger of whom asks the father for his inheritance now, before the father dies, that he may go off on his own to party with his friends and live as he chooses. After a wild fling and losing all the money he had been so generously given by his father, the spendthrift son barely survives and turns to caring for pigs and eating the scraps they leave behind. Finally, in desperation, the son thinks of his father's servants, who all live better than he and wonders if he dare return. He will ask his father to treat him as a hired hand, since he no longer deserves to be called a son. But as Jesus points out, while the son is still a far way off, the father spots him and this insulted, betrayed father totally forgets himself and runs down the road to meet him. Luke describes the father's heart as *rechem*—full of compassion for his much-loved but lost son. Before the son can say anything, the father embraces him, calls for robes to be put around him, a ring on his finger, and the best calf prepared for a feast. When the older brother learns the reason for all the festivities, he sulks at seeing the younger, unloving son's unconditional welcome home. He refuses to go into the party, choosing rather to drown in loathsome comparisons, sure that he has never had such a fuss made over him. Once again, the father responds to the older son from the same *rechem* heart of outpoured love—no withholding. The loving father explains to the elder son that he is always with him and "all that I have is yours." There is more than enough room in the father's *rechem* heart for both the son who foolishly betrayed him and the one who arrogantly compares and insists on his own superior worth. What the father longs for is that both sons might take on the disposition of his heart as their own. He freely offers it to them both. The choice remains theirs.

Certainly this parable found only in Luke's gospel is not without the evangelist's clear intention to demonstrate what the *rechem* heart of God looks like. Jesus knows of what he speaks, since this is his own heart, this very heart of God, now made visible again in the loving and forgiving heart of a Middle Eastern father, who forgets totally his own patriarchal status, to give himself selflessly away for the sake of another, his wayward son. The significance of this father's self-forgetfulness and humility was not lost on the amazed crowds who listened to Jesus speak. His story was all the more compelling because Jesus lived the message that he preached.

Jesus freely let go of his own divinity to become totally one with us. Wherever he went, people discovered that they too were loved, healed, forgiven, and welcomed home in and by Jesus.

The second occasion when the heart of another human person is identified with the same *rechem* heart of God—other than Jesus—occurs in chapter 10 of Luke's gospel. Jesus is asked a question by an uncanny teacher of the Jewish law, who knows well that the law commands them to love their neighbor as they love God. "Who then is my neighbor?" the lawyer asks. Ah, once again it's time for Jesus to use a story to teach the lesson. This time the primary character belongs to an outsider group. Expect some turning of conventional thinking upside down. Jesus has a knack for doing this, especially with so-called leaders of the people. The story opens with a man who has fallen victim to robbers as he was walking from Jerusalem to Jericho. He was left there, bleeding and half-dead, by the side of the road. Both a priest and a Levite, important figures in the Jewish community, pass by the dying man, and never cross the road to care for him in any way. But a Samaritan, whose people are despised by the Jews for their intermarrying customs, sees the injured man and, as Jesus notes, "His heart is moved by compassion" for the forsaken man. The Samaritan goes to him, binds up his wounds, pours oil on them, lifts him on his beast of burden, and takes him to an inn for help, willing to do whatever it costs to care for him. As Jesus concludes the story, he looks at his listeners and asks the lawyer who had first put the question to him: "Who, in your opinion, is neighbor to the one who fell among robbers?" With little wiggle room, the lawyer is forced to respond: "The one, I guess, who showed mercy on him." "Go and do likewise," is Jesus's compelling response, still echoing down the centuries.[4]

The *rechem* heart of the "good Samaritan," a heart reflective of the God in whose image all are created, is the same heart in Jesus, which sends us all to "Go and do likewise." Take care of each other sums it up—regardless of the cost.

---

[4]See Luke 10: 25–37 for the entire passage.

The poet Hafiz understood genuine love in a similar way: "And love says, 'I will, I will take care of you,' to everything that is near."[5] Martin Luther King Jr. recounts the Good Samaritan story with significant levels of reflection. He notices that when both the priest and Levite encounter the man who had fallen among the robbers, they stop and ask themselves, "What will happen to me if I stop to help this person in need?" But when the Samaritan beholds the same person in distress, he asks: "What will happen to this person in need if I do not stop to help?"[6] Hmmm. Compassion thinks first of the other, with little regard for the self—freely poured-out love. Such is the heart of God, the heart of Jesus, and all who, like Jesus, grow in God's likeness.

Compassion as Love Poured Out for Others without Counting the Cost

But the story of Jesus, our forerunner in faith, does not end on the hillside feeding the hungry crowds or by the lakeshore telling parables about God's reign. Jesus's life story ultimately brings him to the hill of Calvary, where he gives his very life for the love of all without exception. For his followers and for his executioners alike, his life is poured out for the life of the world. From the pierced side of Jesus, the water of compassion flows freely, overcoming evil with forgiving love and overcoming death with life eternal. In the Crucified and Risen Jesus, we see God incarnate, revealed as *rechem* love—a love that draws all things to deepest life

---

[5]Hafiz, *The Gift: Poems by Hafiz,* 333.

[6]Martin Luther King Jr., "I've Been to the Mountaintop," final speech delivered April 3, 1968, Memphis, TN. From the time Martin Luther King Jr. became pastor of Dexter Baptist Church in Atlanta in 1954 until his death on April 4, 1968, he incorporated this lesson from Luke's gospel, "On Being a Good Neighbor," into his sermons. See, for example, his sermon of November 20, 1955, at the Dexter Baptist Church and his sermon preached at Ebenezer Baptist Church on May 3, 1964. The text of this speech can be found in King's original handwritten script of thirty-two pages at www.thekingcenter.org/archives. In the eleven-page typed text, this quote appears on page 6.

in the very Heart/Womb of God, whose image we bear. Jesus wore our human flesh to show us the way to live and love as God. Jesus is our forerunner in faith—where he has gone, how he loves, is the pattern for all of us, all who bear the seed of God, compassion's DNA, within us. The mystery and scandal of the Cross is central to compassion as poured-out womb love. In Bernard Lonergan's Thesis 17 on the Incarnation, he offers three points to help us understand what he calls "The Law of the Cross." In less technical language, I explain his points this way: (1) Evil exists which we both experience and participate in. Acknowledging both parts of evil's existence is key to becoming compassionate. Evil is both inside us as well as outside; we cause it as well as suffer from it. For this reason Jesus took on the sins of others as his own. If we cannot wear the evil as part of us, we can never feel with the other as one like us. (2) Jesus took on the evil and said: "Let the evil stop here. I will not pass it on; it will not get beyond me." Jesus absorbed the evil into himself like a sponge. Compassion's test invites us to do the same—to take in evil, but to refuse to return evil for evil. *Let the evil stop here.* Jesus's example becomes our model. Thus, compassion proves stronger than evil. (3) God blessed the self-gift of Jesus, his total love poured out for others, all others, no exception, and God raises Jesus to new life. Here in the resurrection, new life is the gift received in our willingness to die for love. Jesus is God's womb-love in the flesh all the way through death to Risen Life.[7] The mystery or law of the cross is integral to a life in communion with God and others. The willingness to die for love is compassion's linchpin.

In her beautiful work *The Risen Christ,* Caryll Houselander explains the unimaginable gift and call we've been given in the Crucified and Risen Christ: "We are the resurrection going on always, always giving Christ's life back

---

[7]Bernard Lonergan, SJ, "Thesis XVII: The Law of the Cross," in *De Verbo Incarnato* (Rome: Gregorian Pontifical University, 1961), 502–36.

to the world."[8] But are we doing this? I so love and care about the young people I teach. It pains me that many of them feel that they have not experienced this kind of loving among the Christian adults they meet in their everyday encounters. I know some of this can be their own failure to notice the good that surrounds them. But I'm afraid that much of the failure lies with us, who do not take seriously our call to give Christ's life of poured-out love back to the world. How many people feel in our presence, as they did around Jesus—safe, sheltered, healed, and forgiven? Carrie Newcomer sings a song called "Sanctuary" in which she asks "Will you be my refuge, my haven in the storm? Will you keep the embers warm when my fire's all but gone? . . . In a state of true believers, on streets called us and them, it's gonna take some time till the world feels safe again. Will you . . . be my sanctuary till I can carry on?"[9]

Compassion Provides Safe Shelter to Hold One Another in Hard Times

Remembering the connection between *rechem* and womb-love, I think once again of the womb's capacity to expand—to hold life, to protect and shelter it. Yes, we are to be sanctuaries to hold each other, those around us, those who have gone before us, and those who will follow. This is our nature, our true identity. Just last Sunday, I felt so fortunate to attend a liturgy with a priest homilist who passionately wanted his hearers to meet the Jesus, Crucified and Risen, who loved each of them unconditionally. The gospel was a postresurrection account of Jesus's coming through a locked door to find his frightened followers, those guys who had abandoned and denied him before his death, despite all the love and fidelity Jesus had shown them

---

[8] Caryll Houselander, *The Risen Christ* (New York: Sheed and Ward, 1958), 8.

[9] Carrie Newcomer, "Sanctuary," from *The Beautiful Not Yet* (Available Light Records, 2016), track 6.

throughout their years with him. This Jesus came to bring them not condemnation but "peace," to ignite the embers of their love, so smothered by fear and discouragement. Once again, the Risen Jesus longed to be their sanctuary and to help them carry on. They had nothing to fear.

To illustrate this unconditional love that will find a way to break through our resistance—no matter what doors we might bar to try to keep it out—Father Dennis O'Donnell told the story of a good friend of his: A wise and loving father, this man had a conversation with each of his sons, just around their thirteenth birthdays. To each he shared one word, "SANCTUARY," and begged them not to forget it. Then he continued: "You are about to enter an important time in your life, your teen years. And you are going to make mistakes as you try out new things and try to find out who you are as a young man. Some of those mistakes may even have consequences that will frighten you and make you want to hide. When that happens, please. . . . Come to me and say only "SANCTUARY" and I will know. You can sit there in the silence, and I will keep you sheltered by a love that will never let you go, no matter what you did. We will get through it together. I want you to know this now, and to count on it, when you feel despondent, like a failure, and want to run away. I will be your SANCTUARY—till you can carry on."

The Freedom to Give Ourselves as Gift

In the gospel of John, that long, theological statement about who Jesus is as "The Word Become Flesh" (Jn 1), the gospel writer makes it clear that no one takes Jesus's life from him. No, he freely lays it down, gives it up. The freedom of God to love is preeminent. Love must be freely given to be love. *Rechem* love is freely outpoured—no holding back. Only freedom has power to overcome our fear. Whether it's a teenage boy afraid to tell his father about the terrible mistake he made, or fearful disciples of Jesus hiding away in an Upper Room after their leader's death, for fear that they might be next, fear keeps us from loving freely. It takes a lifetime to grow free, but this is the journey on which we are here to help each other. We are the road to each other's freedom and their sanctuary along the way.

In a most helpful work, titled *The Art of Passing Over,* Francis Dorff offers a psychological explanation of how human persons grow toward freedom as they move through three basic fears: (1) the fear of having something to prove; (2) the fear of having something to hide; and (3) the fear of having something to lose.[10] Growth through these fears has a normative chronological trajectory, though it's rare that people leave the fear behind entirely. Each fear can rear its ugly head anytime in our life journey. It might be helpful to get in touch with each of them inside yourself to assess the impact each has on your freedom at present. Then imagine the feeling of being able to let go of each of these fears and to stand before the world just as we are—free and loving.

By moving through and beyond the fear that I have something to prove—to prove that I am good enough, smart enough, beautiful enough—whatever it is that is my greatest nagging concern, the one that tells me that I am simply not enough, freedom comes as grace to let this go and to stand before the world empty and free to say: "Here I am; I have nothing to prove." I am free to accept myself exactly as I am with all my gifts and limitations, all my strengths and weaknesses. I have no desire to prove anything to anyone; I have only the desire to become the best version of myself. Taste the joy of this great freedom. Pray for its grace and work toward knowing its fruit in you. Receive the help of those who companion you along your way.

The second fear grips me with a need to cover up because I have something to hide. This fear mounts with time's pass-

---

[10]Francis Dorff, *The Art of Passing Over: An Invitation to Living Creatively* (Mahwah, NJ: Paulist Press, 1988), 152–62.

ing and the accumulation of mistakes and regrets. The fear of needing to hide all these unwanted parts of my life from others imprisons me. Freedom comes as the gift to be able to stand before the world in my beauty and brokenness, and know deep within that I have nothing to hide. This is the grace God so longs for me to discover: I am loved just as I am, and this grace frees me to love others in their vulnerable, incomplete lives as well.

Finally, the third fear is that I have something to lose. Throughout life, this fear takes various forms, from losing my good reputation, to my social status in work or society, from losing my health and economic security, to the loss of my loved ones. Ultimately, I am unfree because of the fear of losing my very life. Such fear of dying actually prevents me from living life here and now to the fullest. My highest, human freedom is achieved when I am willing to let go of it all, even my very life. Herein, the great paradox of finding my life only in losing it is lived out. Jesus is the paradigm for growing totally free. Jesus's measure of becoming fully human is God's great desire for all of us. Such freedom is reflected in the prayer Ignatius of Loyola passed on to all who rely on his spiritual guidance today. That we might grow into God's free and loving children, Ignatius taught us to pray: "Take, Lord, receive all my liberty, my memory, understanding, my entire will. . . . You have given all to me, now I return it. Give me only Your love and Your grace, that's enough for me." Even the desire to pray this prayer is grace itself—a gift given to us. It's never our own achievement.

But we are here to help one another. We can do this for one another, because we are being held in this tender place by the God who is our refuge, our shelter from the storm, until our fears subside and the world is a safe place again. Yes, this is who we are capable of being for our sons, our daughters, our sisters and brothers—those neighbors Jesus asks us to take care of by the side of the road.

God in Jesus Is Counting on Us to Become Who We Are

The thought of Jesus entrusting to us the capacity to love like him reminds me of an old story in which the author imagines Jesus's return to heaven after his Ascension. The story goes something like this:

The Angel Gabriel met Jesus at the gate of heaven after he completed his mission on earth. "Well done, Jesus!" Gabriel proclaimed. "You have saved the world, loving all without condition or exception even to the point of death—a love that was simply too much—too forgiving, too merciful, too all-embracing—for many to accept, but you accomplished it." Jesus only smiled and said: "Yes, Thank you." But, Gabriel went on: "What's going to happen now? How will the work of healing and loving the world continue?" Jesus looked up and answered calmly. "I have left that to Peter and John, to Mary, Martha and the rest. They will go on loving and taking care of all without exception." "But, suppose Peter gets too busy with his nets and Martha with her household chores to remember your saving work of compassion and mercy toward all. What then?" Gabriel asked. Jesus said nothing for a long moment and then softly spoke: "I have not made other plans. I am counting on them."[11]

Jesus is counting on us to love and take care of all without exception. He never asked us to preserve a doctrine or argue about ritual practices, about who gets to do what or stand

[11]Adapted from an old legend I found online at some point. It was attributed to a person named "Goven," from an article entitled, "The Calling," in 1934. The final lines "I have not made other plans. I am counting on them," come back to me often.

where. He seems much more interested that everyone feel included, welcomed, forgiven, restored, and empowered to believe that they too can love as they have been loved. We have a lot of loving to do. Jesus is counting on us.

Conversation Starters

1. *Can you remember a time when you felt within you a compassion tug to go out of yourself for the sake of another?*
2. *Are there ways in which stories of Jesus's compassion, recounted here or in the gospels, have inspired you to "go and do likewise"? What other lessons might Jesus's hearers (and we ourselves) take from Jesus's choice of an outcast to bear God's heart, while important Jewish leaders missed the chance to resemble the One they taught about?*
3. *How does the pattern of Jesus's life reveal the height and depth of God's boundless love for you, for all?*

PART II

COMPASSION AS THE DNA
OF OUR HUMAN BECOMING

*Learning Compassion
through the Rechem Hearts of Others*

3

Learning Compassion
from My Dad's Big Heart

The Heart of Jesus Passed on to Us

It seems evident to me that those who love us pass on their legacy of loving, counting on us to carry that love forward. I leave it to you to reflect on how true this is for you. As you look into your own life experience, I invite you to consider who has worn that face of selfless, outpoured love for you? On whose shoulders do you now stand, realizing that you are to create space for others to stand on your shoulders today or someday? Before I focus on lessons about compassion that I learned, and am still learning, from my dad's legacy, I'd like to linger a little longer on the life of Jesus, in whom the gospels tell us the living God of compassion took flesh. The last chapter closed with a story of Jesus's counting on us, his followers, to carry on his legacy, his life and message of compassion for all. And he promised to be with us, so that we would not be doing this compassion work alone. The greatest gift in my own life is to experience this presence of Jesus for myself. The Spirit of the Risen Christ that has been handed over to us makes it possible for us to encounter Christ with us today and to experience his humanity in a personally concrete though subtle way. It is sight offered by faith, a kind of heart-vision.

At times in my life, seeing Jesus as my brother has provided a cherished image for me. I have vivid memories, some
still going on in the present, of my three brothers hoisting
their children (now they do it with grandchildren) up on
their shoulders to carry them through the streets, up the hill,
or at a sporting event to get a better view of something that
their size prevented them from seeing. They always seemed
to have the best seat in the house! I've often prayed with
that image and asked my brother Jesus to put me on his
shoulders so I could see further when things in my life feel
muddled or confused, so that I could feel less tired when
life seems burdensome, or simply so that I could know that
I am being carried when I feel alone.

The Spirit's gift empowers me to see the face of God in
the face of others as we continue to grow the Body of Christ
to full stature. I hope that I've participated in some of this
Body-building as well, by hoisting others up and offering
my shoulders for them to rest upon. More than that, I hope
to be there as this carrying place in the future. I have often
marveled at Jesus's assurance in the gospel of John that
if we believe in him, we will do the work he has done. In
fact, Jesus says, "Whoever believes in Me will do the work
that I do and will do greater ones than these" (Jn 14:12).
Imagine—for this, Jesus is counting on us!

The Gift of Being Counted On

The Apostle Paul emphatically told his beloved friends
in Philippi that the pattern of Jesus's life must become the
pattern for theirs. We who claim to see in Jesus the face of
compassion are asked to put on his mind and heart. That
rechem heart of the Good Samaritan ought to describe ours
as well. I keep remembering that God is counting on us to
make love visible in the world today, just as Jesus did in his
day. He is simply the firstborn in whose footsteps we follow.

There is something about being counted on that keeps

me going when I might otherwise lose heart. My nephews tell me that their young children make them want to be better human beings, for sure. I remember my brother Frank musing one time about an experience he had at the grocery checkout counter with my young nephew Frankie, who was about eleven at the time. My brother had paid for the items and was putting away the change when he noticed that the young clerk had given him an extra twenty dollar bill. "Oh, it looks like you gave me an extra twenty," my brother remarked, smiling. "You'll probably need it later when you're justifying your cash register." The young woman was noticeably flustered, but grateful, to have the money returned. "That was really cool, Dad," my nephew said proudly, as they were leaving the store. As my brother recounted the incident, he wondered aloud, "Would I have been so quick to give it back, if Frankie had not been with me? I can only hope so." The truth is: doing good for the sake of others is always a healthy motivator, a godly instinct. God has given us to one another to help save us. It goes on all the time.

I've heard others tell me similar things, even students I teach now. "As the first one in my family to go to college, I feel a responsibility to set an example for my younger sister and brother. They are counting on me," Raevon, a young college student, told me recently. I suspect strongly that this same motivation kept my father going when he might have otherwise become discouraged by some of life's burdens and setbacks, of which he had his fair share. My dad learned that real love, selfless love, suffered and endured. He wanted us to know this too.

Seeing with the Eyes of the Heart

My dad was born in County Sligo, Ireland, but came to the United States as a young man after the death of his mother, and with the hope of sending money back home to his father, brothers, and sisters. There are many facts about my dad's early life I don't know. We often say that we wish, as kids, we had listened more attentively to his stories and learned more about his younger years on the farm in Sligo. But when I think of my dad, as I often do, it's not about the historical details of his life, though those events and circumstances provided the way for his "big, compassionate heart" to peer through. That's what I think of most—the way my dad saw the world and everyone in it through his great, big heart. In my dad's own simple, unassuming way, he taught me so much about the *rechem* heart of God.

My father was a man of deep faith, unswerving hope, and selfless love, but he showed it in the most ordinary, unpretentious ways. I'm certain I missed many lessons he offered, but I'm grateful for the ones I cherish and from which I continue to learn. I think the secret lies in savoring the memories—spending time lingering over the little things. If you're able to discover goodness, beauty, love in the small things of life, my dad might have something to say to you, as well. For most of us, the ordinary is all we have to work with. Let me share a few of the compassion lessons I learned from my dad's less than sensational life.

For more than forty years, my dad worked for the PTC—the Philadelphia Transportation Company, today's SEPTA.[1] My father did not drive a bus or trolley, but he fixed them. Each day he stood on the corner waiting for one to take him from our house in Drexel Hill, a suburb of Philadelphia, to 69th Street and then home again in the afternoon. When my dad arrived home each evening, we counted on him to have a story or two about his day. More often than not, the day's story would involve someone he had met—someone who had come into the shop, the guys with whom he had had lunch, someone he engaged in

---

[1]Southeastern Pennsylvania Transportation Authority.

conversation while waiting for the trolley, or someone he saw and chatted with during the ride. Inevitably my dad would end his story of the person he encountered with a brief pause, during which time his eyes often filled up, while he looked intently at us, shook his head ever so slightly, and said softly: "the nicest fella you'd ever ask to meet." As my father pictured the face that rose up to meet him in the recounting of his story of this now-no-longer-stranger, gratitude lit up his face. Each of us somehow bathed in its glow. It did not take long before we realized that my dad ended almost every nightly story with that same line. We could all finish it for him, and we often repeat it to each other today. "Nicest fella you'd ever ask to meet." Gradually, I began to see that my dad's impression of the person he had met that day told us more about my dad, than it did about the person he encountered, as wonderful as he or she might have been. Every daily interaction for my dad was for him a revelation. In the process of facing so many "nicest fellas," he was becoming what he saw in them—the nicest fella you could ever ask to meet. And that's the truth, because "we don't see things as they are; we see things as we are."[2] Because my dad's heart went out to everyone he met in loving-kindness, his strong compassion connection linked him with those he met in ways that brought out the goodness in them as well.

Finding Meaning Hidden in the Ordinary

My father loved butter pecan ice cream and French apple pie. You know the kind with raisins inside and a thin glaze of vanilla icing drizzled across the top. By some maneuver-

---

[2]Anais Nin, *Seduction of the Minotaur* (Chicago: Swallow Press, 1961), 124. Nin recounts these words as an old Talmudic saying. It has been included in many writings, one of which is the best-selling self-help book by Steven R. Covey, *The Seven Habits of Highly Effective People* (New York: Simon and Schuster, 2004), 28.

ing miracle, my mother managed from time to time to hide the last piece of pie from the scavenging hunt of my three brothers, my sister, and myself. This feat accomplished, she would eagerly present it to my dad at dessert time. Without fail, though sometimes to my mom's chagrin, my dad would engage in the ritual act of sharing, that we all knew was coming. "Sure, have a little taste, Cathy," he'd say, with his entreating Irish brogue, which cannot be captured in print. "No thanks, Dad. You eat it," I'd say, as I got older and caught on. "Oh, just try a little bite; it's delicious," he'd continue. I remember the back and forth like it was yesterday.

A similar wave of emotion stirs in me when I picture my father on any given weeknight with the daily newspaper held close to his face. Suddenly, he would look up with his familiar fatherly, but endearing, voice: "Shhhh . . . listen to this story." Then he began to read aloud to all of us. It was usually a human interest story, possibly always of human interest, with a lesson he somehow wanted or even needed to draw from it for all of us. More often than not he would recount the details, as I recall, with tears in his eyes, as for example, a brave firefighter risking his own life to get to the family still inside the burning building, refusing to give up until all were carried to safety. I remember my brother Frank asking him quizzically "But, do you know him, Dad?" "Of course, I don't actually know him," my dad responded. Later, I came to see that at some deeper level of connection, my father did know him—the same compassion gene was operative in both. Did my dad somehow see that all of us have been born from that same womb of love?

As I have relived these childhood memories of my dad throughout my life, I am struck by several meanings of such behavior. My father yearned to give us all that he loved—all that he found worthwhile and good in life. The pie was good; the stories, worthwhile. I certainly could draw on more significant events from which to cull this lesson, but somehow it's these almost insignificant character traits of my dad that keep coming back to me. So often I simply resort to describing my dad as having a really big heart. He seemed to me totally open to life, available, accepting, ultimately abandoned (handed over) . . . but that came a bit later.

Cherishing the Memory of Really Big Hearts

The description of a big heart reminds me of another story I was told by a priest who had recently presided at the funeral of a twenty-six-year-old man who had been killed in a car accident. Father Joe was standing in the back of the church, waiting for the funeral procession to line up, when a woman approached him and introduced herself as Michael's Aunt Helen. She was obviously distraught, as was the rest of Michael's family, including the young woman, soon to be mother of Michael's unborn child. The aunt began to share that Michael's mother and father loved Michael deeply and were heartbroken at his sudden, untimely death. In the midst of their agony, as "good Catholics," they were also worried because Michael no longer went to church, had been living with his girlfriend, and sometimes drank too heavily. "But," Aunt Helen insisted, "he was such a good boy. I wish I could go up to heaven right now, Father. I'd tell God, before he could pass any judgment, that Michael had a really big heart." Father Joe was moved, he said, by this aunt's great love for her nephew and he said in reply:

Where do you think Michael got that really big heart? Don't worry that you need to tell God. The God who loves Michael with a heart bigger than any of us can imagine has already welcomed Michael into that Heart of Boundless Mercy, where Michael's "really big heart" now knows no bounds.

Once we have met this God personally, we can console one another with this assurance of how God loves. But it helps to catch glimpses from people whose love for us, or ours for them, seems almost boundless. Sometimes that becomes clearest when suffering is involved.

When Suffering Births Compassion

A vivid memory comes back to me when I think of compassion's connection with a willingness to suffer. As students entered into a brief period of silence in class one day, I invited them to reflect on how they had encountered something of God's compassion in their own life experience. How did God show up? Bridget was the first to speak. She said:

> As I was sitting here, what came to me so powerfully was the face of my mother. Last year, I contracted a virus which settled in a nerve in my face. The pain was excruciating especially during the long nights. One night when I could hardly bear the pain, I looked up and saw my mother, who kept vigil by my bedside, looking back at me with such a tender, pain-wracked expression on her weary face. I knew in that moment that my mom would give anything, not to bear this pain with me, but to bear it instead of me.

Along with others who listened to Bridget, I could only nod in agreement. She had indeed met the compassion of God wearing the face of her mother.

Is it possible that there is more to be revealed about the character of our hearts when what happens in life seems almost unbearable? Is this how we come to see that compassion knows no bounds? Lines from the Bohemian-Austrian poet Rainer Maria Rilke, hint at his awareness of such "a more"—even beauty—present everywhere. Rilke writes:

Beauty will become paltry if you look for it only in what is pleasing. Surely, it may be found there from time to time. But beauty resides and waits to be uncovered in the one who believes it is present everywhere and who refuses to leave the spot until she has stubbornly coaxed it forth.[3]

To stay with experiences of suffering and loss until we coax the deeper meaning and beauty from them is a challenge that growing in compassion asks of us. Too often, I know I want to run away or forget about the painful parts of loving that include suffering and heartbreak. But I've also come to know that facing our pain, hurt, or difficulty can change us. It can break us open. As a consequence, we are never the same again. Such unsought encounters (you know, those things you never asked to have happen to you—the script you didn't write for your life) beg us to take them in. They entreat us to create a place within our hearts—an inner space, where the suffering we need to face is no longer an object outside us, but a subject within that we behold. We allow this suffering to enter us, to be held with humility, truth, and mercy until it teaches us more about love's fullest meaning. The love that is compassion, God's way of loving, pours itself out as self-gift so that more life may come.

Compassion Gives Itself Away

It's time to say something of how my dad once again helped me learn more about becoming compassionate, as God is compassionate. For so many of us who loved my dad, suffering came in the cruel guise of Alzheimer's disease. Nine years of enduring this disease left my Irish,

---

[3]Rainer Maria Rilke, *The Poet's Guide to Life: The Wisdom of Rilke*, ed. and trans. Ulrich Baer (New York: Random House, 2005), 54.

storytelling dad, this warm and sensitive "nicest fella you'd ever ask to meet" with a mind and body that were unable to respond—powerless to lift even an arm of his own volition. For the last three years of his struggle, he was in a small, private nursing facility. My mother sat with him every day, and we, five siblings, were there often, always on Sundays. One particular Sunday stands out for me. All of us were in the small room at the same time, some kneeling beside the chair where dad was propped up. We patted his face, rubbed his back, and watched this man who had once named us, who no longer seemed to know us at all, let alone our names.

On one of these Sundays, my brother Tom expressed a frustration that might have overcome any of us on another given day. Tom said something like: "I don't know why we even keep coming, week after week. Dad has no idea we're even here. There's absolutely nothing that we can do for him; he's just there." In the face of this apparent darkness and loss, I remember very clearly something rising up in me that said: "You're right, Tom, there seems to be nothing we can do any longer for dad, but, maybe there is something dad still wants to do for us." Quite honestly, I believe that I am still trying to uncover all that dad was doing for me, as I faced his diminishment—his being handed over, abandoning every gift he had been given. One by one, slowly, all that we knew and loved about my dad was taken away from him, right before our eyes. From his lilting Irish laughter, to his loving caring heart, that heart which seemed to make room for everyone: the man he met at the trolley stop, the family in the sad story he read aloud to us in the evening paper, friends who stopped by, for whom he readily jumped up to put on the tea kettle. All of it was given over.

Here's the lesson my dad was offering me, as I've gradually come to claim it: Every gift you have, you will give back sooner or later. So, give yourself away freely now—choose to see all that you have as gift, not as something you've earned that you should cling to as an entitlement.

A Lifetime of Learning to Love as God Loves

Perhaps, you, like me, easily identify with Peter, the disciple Jesus chose to be the "Rock" on which he would build the church. Again, the paradox of the fumbling, impetuous Peter taking on the characteristics of this steady, solid rock seems almost laughable. Yet it's clear too that Peter had a really big heart. He loved Jesus wildly, despite his own weaknesses and self-concern. And it's more than clear that Jesus saw his heart and the *rechem* love of which it was capable. Before John ends his gospel, he shares a conversation between Jesus and Peter in which Peter professes how great his love for Jesus is and that Jesus knows it. The cost of such loving, we hear again, is to share that love with everyone else. Jesus tells Peter, "Feed my sheep." If you love Me, take care of everyone else. Your love, like mine, can have no exceptions, no exclusions. It would take Peter a while to understand just how much loving after God's own heart would ask of him. The Risen Christ continued to teach Peter and us that we will not be able to grow this big a heart all on our own. We must be handed over and given up. Here is the paradox of freedom: only in losing our lives will we find them. In being handed over, we become truly free. "Truly, truly, I say to you, when you were young, you girded yourself and walked where you would; but when you are old, you will stretch out your hands and another will gird you and carry you where you do not wish to go. . . . And after this Jesus said, 'Follow Me' " (Jn 21:15–19). These lines give me much to ponder as I realize the work God still wants to do in me to help me become who I am created to be: another face of compassion. But for what other purpose do I or you live? Love has given us life. Freely we have received; freely we are to give back.

The Freedom to Let Go

Only after my dad's death did a story he used to tell come back to me with deeper meaning. My dad's stories often grew by leaps and bounds, depending on the lesson he was trying to teach. They were all true in some deeper sense of the word. This one begins with some things that actually happened. I love telling it with a hint of my father's brogue, but you can only mimic this in reading for yourselves. Give it a try!

Ohhhh, Uncle Patty had a wonderful life with Aunt Kate and the six beautiful children they raised on their farm in Sligo. He loved them all—his dear wife, Kate, their six children and many grandchildren, and the land he farmed those many years. When Patty was close to death, the entire family gathered around his bed; Kate brushed his brow tenderly and asked if there was anything else she could get for him. There is one thing, Patty whispered to Kate. "Will you go out to the field, bring me in a little piece of sod and put it here in my hand? Within a few short hours, with prayers echoing around his bedside, with Kate's loving kiss upon his brow, and with his clump of Irish sod in his hand, Uncle Patty went home to God.

(No, this is not the end of the story!) . . . At the pearly gates, Uncle Patty is greeted by St. Peter, who welcomes him warmly and is ready to let him in, when he spots something in his right hand. "What is that you're clinging to, Patty," Peter asks? "Sure, it's me Irish sod," quips Uncle Patty. "Well you'll have to drop it," Peter retorts quickly. "We all return to God empty-handed." "Oh, I'll never let go of this," Patty says in his strong, determined way. "Then there's no going into heaven for you, Patty."

Outside those pearly gates, Uncle Patty sat and sat and sat. Years passed and many, many a loving person entered into heavenly bliss, while Patty sat outside clinging to that piece of Sligo sod he would not give up. Eventually, Patty's granddaughter, little Katie herself, died and arrived there beside him at the gates of heaven. When Katie spotted her grand-dad after all these years, she rushed to hug him and in the embrace, yes, that piece of sod slipped from Patty's fist and they both found themselves on the other side. What do you think Uncle Patty saw there to his great, bewildered surprise? Gone was his piece of sod, but there before his wondering eyes, Patty beheld, with amazement, the entire Emerald Isle.

Maybe this lesson of letting go, which my dad lived in more convincing ways than the story he told, is the reason why I love these lines from the poet Wendell Berry.

> No, no, there's no going back.
> Less and less you are
> that possibility you were.
> More and more you have become
> those lives and deaths
> that have belonged to you . . .
> Now more than ever, you can be generous
> toward each day that comes, young,
> to disappear forever, and yet remain
> unaging in the mind.
> Every day you have less reason
> not to give yourself away.[4]

Yes, it seems clear to me that the more of ourselves we give away, the bigger our heart grows and the more we become

---

[4]Wendell Berry, "1993, #1," in *A Timbered Choir: The Sabbath Poems, 1979–1997* (Washington, DC: Counterpoint, 1998), 167.

who we are meant to be. I smile each time I eat a piece of apple pie and remember my dad. More than that, I am grateful every time I meet a person and the thought rises up in me "the nicest fella you'd ever ask to meet." That thought not only reminds me of my dad; it gives me hope that he lives on in me. What a great gift!

Conversation Starters

1. *This chapter invites us to ponder ordinary events and people in our lives who have lessons in compassion to teach. Can you recall any people or events in your life that have taught you similar lessons?*
2. *No one wants or asks for suffering in life. Has there been a particular experience of suffering which you now understand as holding a lesson for you that you might not have learned any other way?*
3. *Is there a particular line or story from this chapter that resonates in you, making some kind of compassion connection?*
4. *What value do you see in learning to let go?*

4

Learning Compassion from the Broken Hearts of Rwandan Widows and Others

Finding Myself in Rwanda and Rwanda in Me

My dad was not alive by the time I went to Rwanda. But in many ways, he provided the inner impulse for me to go there, and I have no doubt that he companioned me on those hills—hills that in many ways resembled those of the Ireland he loved so well. There were times I felt my dad's presence so keenly that I sensed that my tears had their source in his eyes.[1]

My journey to Rwanda took place during a 2005–6 sabbatical. I spent a semester there, gathering stories for research I was doing on forgiveness and reconciliation. It may seem strange, even unlikely, that a small country, on a continent we too often ignore, could have life lessons to teach the rest of us in the developed, highly educated, and affluent West. Why spend a scholarly, research sabbatical there, for God's sake? Yet I felt strongly that I was being called to go to Rwanda for God's sake and for mine. I was

---

[1] Abraham Joshua Heschel, *The Ineffable Name of God: Man* (New York: Continuum, 2007). In this lovely book of poems, Heschel expresses a similar thought: "From your eyes drips a tear, its source in me" ("I and You," 31).

not disappointed. What I remember most clearly upon my return was people asking me what I was doing in Rwanda, and spontaneously the reply rose up in me: The question is rather, "What is Rwanda doing in me?" I trust that Rwanda continues to work its salvific power in me.

Here's a little background on the country and its people that may help you enter their stories, find something of yourself in them. By now, I hope you can say with me that they are also our people. Who they are has something to say about who we are, or who we can become. During the hundred-day genocide of 1994, the Rwandan people suffered through some of the worst evils we humans are capable of doing to each other. Yet in so many of the Rwandan people, the incredible goodness of which we humans are capable was likewise revealed. In the face of evil, many chose to put on the face of love. But that decision to choose love came at a cost.

For several years prior to going to Rwanda, I had been studying contemporary theories on forgiveness—on healing life's wounds from theological and psychological perspectives, but I wanted to meet and learn from people who had chosen to walk the talk. Who were the Rwandan people I had read about who were risking the long, rough journey to forgive and reconcile after the atrocities of genocide, when the expected, predictable route pointed toward more violence, retaliation, and vengeance? Was the country as a whole attempting to break that unbroken chain of violence that keeps so many of us bound by a past we cannot change? One war after another seems to have its source in past wrongs suffered without the offended ones being able to even the score. But isn't the unbroken chain of evil proof enough that the score is never evened, that the cycle of violence goes on in a tit-for-tat fashion often from one generation to the next?[2] Could this humble, little country

---

[2]Some of the significant voices speaking out and writing about our need to break the chain of violence in our world are Lewis Smedes, Johann Christophe

teach an arrogant, big world how to break that cycle of retaliation by an alternative choice? That choice must be made one person at a time. Hopefully, world leaders will be moved by the will of the people.

Rwanda is a powerful example of a social factor we cannot ignore—the role of the media in shaping the attitudes and beliefs of a people. In our contemporary situation, half a world away and a quarter century later, think about the influence of social media on how we see the world and our human family. In studying the conditions that made the horrors of the Rwandan genocide possible, I found fear-breeding propaganda to be the number one toxic force filling people's minds and hearts. A favorite radio station blasted threats night and day warning the dominant (85 percent) Hutu population that the Tutsis (15 percent minority) were going to overtake them, as they had earlier in their postcolonial history. To protect themselves and their country, the Hutus were told, they needed to rise up and kill every Tutsi while there was still time. Extermination of the Tutsi people, even the unborn, was touted as the only way for the majority of the Rwandan people, the Hutus, to be safe. Suddenly, neighbors, even family members, were to be feared and hated. Thinking of the Tutsis as friends, neighbors, or even human beings would prevent good people from carrying out the work the media was inciting them to do in the name of their beloved Rwanda. Day after day, the Tutsis were referred to as cockroaches (*inenzi*), which needed to be trampled underfoot for the good of all. The airwaves resounded the message, and fear and evil spread like an infectious disease. For many ordinary Hutu people who participated in harmful acts and/or massive violence during the genocide, their abhorrent behavior demonstrated all too tragically the effects of social contagion.

In my personal conversations with many Rwandan

Arnold, Everett Worthington, Michael McCullough, Desmond Tutu, and John Paul Lederach.

Christians and in their prison testimonies, they confessed remorsefully that throughout those months of 1994, their ethnic blood boiled up in them more powerfully than the waters of their baptism. If evil and violence have a social component, where a pull toward evil can negatively affect the moral fabric of a whole people, where is its alternate counter-pull? Christians, who believe in the resurrection of Jesus, base our faith in the utter incapacity of evil to have the last word. Love and goodness will always prove the stronger. But we need to do our part; to nurture a culture of love, trust, forgiveness, and compassion.

As I journeyed through the hills of Rwanda, I found myself flooded by a grace I can only name as compassion. It filled the personal, tragic stories shared by countless widows and orphans, women religious, and repentant prisoners, which gave them hope and a chance to live again. I would like to give you a chance to meet a few of those children, women, and men who have become my greatest teachers of compassion. In their broken-open hearts, I saw love—emptied out, removing the need for enemies, as forgiveness and reconciliation found a way to heal their hearts, restore their families, and save the future of their beloved country.

A Bequest from the Slain Rwandan Children

I am profoundly grateful to the beautiful but slain children of Rwanda, innocent victims of the genocide of 1994, who shared with me a haunting bequest. While visiting the Children's Wing of the Genocide Memorial Center in Kigali, Rwanda, I stopped before the shrine-like stations dedicated to each slaughtered child. Mementos of their toys and clothing, words they last spoke, their favorite food, their simple joys and hopes—most particularly photos of their young, beautiful faces flooded my mind and heart as I prayed before each sacred encounter with life and death. The incredible ache of holding so much intense pain caused me to look away, but each time I tried to do so, I glanced down to the brochure in my hand that I had picked up at the entrance to the Children's Center. Alongside an old, discarded sneaker and photo of a young boy, were the words now emblazoned in my heart and conscience: "If you had known me, and if you had known yourself, you would never have killed me."[3]

Over time, this mantra has evolved for me from a lament for the past horror, one requiring deep and profound mourning and repentance, to a loving bequest for a new and reconciled future. In honor of and in union with these innocent Rwandan children, will we resolve to do as they entreat us? "Yes, I will try to come to know the other and, in the process, come to know myself . . . so that, in truth, it will become impossible for me to harm another person." The compassion link transcends space and time. This question extends to each of us: Do you believe that there are no strangers? We are one. There's just us; there is no "them." I find myself making this compassion promise and turning to others to help me keep it.[4]

Coming to See Myself in the Other and the Other in Me

That first Other to help me keep this promise is Jesus himself, whose own life as God among us provides the way for me to follow. In His Sacred Heart, I see more clearly my own need to know myself better. A poem of Denise Levertov discloses the incredible marvel that is the Mystery of the Incarnation. In this mystery, I place my trust—trust

---

[3]Brochure from the Children's Center of the Kigali Genocide Museum, Kigali, Rwanda. The Children's Center opened in 2004.

[4]Since returning from Rwanda, I have given numerous presentations with photos of Rwandan children accompanying this actual brochure. The faces of these innocent children with their piercing eyes, their outstretched arms and their captivating smiles call us to live this bequest. I have often heard a promise in turn resounding from a receptive audience, summoned by such vulnerable faces, to try to follow this entreaty.

that I will come to recognize in every creature (tainted but God-sought, like me) a brother or a sister.

> It's when we face for a moment
> the worst our kind can do, and shudder to know
> the taint in our own selves, that awe
> cracks the mind's shell and enters the heart:
> not to a flower; not to a dolphin,
> to no innocent form
> but to this creature, vainly sure
> it and no other is god-like, God
> (out of compassion for our ugly
> failure to evolve) entrusts,
> as guest, as brother,
> The Word.[5]

A significant source of help to evolve came for me from the Rwandan people who survived the massacre, and even some who contributed to it. During my three months journeying through the lush and lovely country, I had the privilege of meeting even lovelier people. Twelve years earlier, Rwanda had been almost decimated—over one million Rwandan Tutsis and moderate Hutus slaughtered by Rwandan radical Hutus in less than one hundred days. In the aftermath of such unspeakable atrocities, hundreds of survivors who shared their stories with me recounted their fear and revulsion on first peering into the face of the hated other—those who had killed members of their family during the war. How could they bear to see the face of evil looking back at them in the once familiar faces of long-time neighbors turned killers, trusted friends who pillaged and destroyed everything they valued and loved?

I met people who, no less horrifying, recognized them-

---

[5]Denise Levertov, "On the Mystery of the Incarnation," in *The Stream and the Sapphire* (New York: New Directions, 1997), 19.

selves in and as the distorted face of evil, a tortured face that now looked out into the world, back upon themselves, and into the face of other persons as an object of their hatred and contempt. But what was most incredible in my experience of so many Rwandan people, from both sides of this demonic engagement, was their eventual response to such a confrontation. Rather than returning evil for evil, these people found a way, little by little, to transform evil's countenance, in themselves and in the other, into a face of forgiving/forgiven and reconciling love. They became compassion. What was it that they came to discover about themselves and about the other that enabled such a transformation? How did they come to see beyond evil to goodness, beyond hatred to love, beyond death to life? From many of my Rwandan friends, I learned the same lesson. They came to realize that their very capacity to live again depended on how they responded to the other and vice versa.

Speciosa, a Tutsi woman who had lost thirty-two family members including her husband, four children, her mother, father, and several siblings, was so weighed down by inner turmoil following their brutal deaths that she was unable to raise her eyes even to look at a Hutu. In every one of them, she saw a terrifying animal—a monster whom she despised. As she was being eaten up by rage and vengeance, Speciosa struggled to find some inner calm in prayer. Retreating to the stillness of her parish church, she sought refuge and a semblance of peace. Little by little, Speciosa began to feel deep within that God still loved her, despite her intense feelings of hatred. Could it be possible, she wondered somewhat awestruck, that if God still loved her despite her hatred, that God loved the Hutus as well? Was God big enough to hold them both? The question lingered and began to change her. As she pondered and prayed, Speciosa recounts that something shifted inside her. The womb of love seemed to expand. Thus, she began to see the Hutus differently. Rather than inhuman monsters, she started to recognize in each face another grieving, shame-filled human being like herself. She saw herself in them, she said, and a God who held them all with forgiveness and compassion. Speciosa's awakening to a shared humanity, recognized in a divinely loved brokenness, initiated her long journey to forgive and reconcile with every one of them. Her journey has gone far beyond forgiving those Hutus who directly killed her family members.

As a member of Les Bons Samaritains, Speciosa is committed to help mend and reconcile the entire Rwandan people and her beloved country. Grounded in the lesson taught by the parable of the Good Samaritan, whose heart resembled Jesus's own *rechem* love, hundreds of Hutus and Tutsis move together across borders of enmity and division to bring to each person they meet the face of unconditional mercy and love. Over and over again in villages, marketplaces, churches, and prisons throughout Rwanda, I met these Bons Samaritains.[6] In their faces, young and old, victims and perpetrators, I met compassion in the flesh once more, a compassion stronger than evil and death that broke through their own experience of deadness. In coming to know the other, as a wounded yet lovable human being, they found themselves and new life.

There was Clebert, a prison guard, who had spent years treating the prisoners, mostly Hutus accused of killing or looting during the genocide, with utter disdain and cruelty. In his eyes, these prisoners had given up any claim to human decency and so fully merited the disregard in which he held them. But Clebert discovered that his own hardened heart began softening over time, as he witnessed the loving presence and fidelity of the Bons Samaritains. These women and

---

[6]Founded in 1986 by Emmanuel Munyangendo and Anne Marie Mukankurango, Les Bons Samaritains have been an effective agent in bridging the massive divide between the two Rwandan ethnic groups—the Hutu and the Tutsi—since the genocide of 1994.

men, like Speciosa, came weekly to the prison to share their personal stories of pain and brokenness and to bring the message of God's unconditional love and mercy (*rechem*) for each and every one of them, regardless of their past wrong-doings. As Clebert watched prisoners undergo undeniable changes in their attitudes and behavior, he began to reflect on his own life—his bitterness, cynicism, and lack of compassion. He began to see that the disdain he had for others was, in truth, a reflection of his own lack of self-regard. His first impressions of these Bons Samaritains, as crazy people with a naïve outlook on healing the world through love and forgiveness, gave way to amazement at the change taking place right before his eyes. When he felt a yearning inside himself to let go of his own self-righteousness, he literally fell to his knees in humility and repentance. From a skeptical observer to a faithful member of Les Bons Samaritains, Clebert has come to understand that in crossing borders into another's life, especially the life of a stranger or outcast, he discovered more about himself as well as the other. The other, even a condemned prisoner, is like him though other than him: a human being infinitely worthy of respect. In forgiving them and regarding them with respect, he learned to see himself forgiven through the respect with which the prisoners beheld him.

When Edithe arrived at the Assumption Sisters' secondary school in 2003 in Birambo, Rwanda, she was sixteen. She carried with her the enormous pain of loss. Her mother, father, brother, and baby sister were all victims of the genocide, which left Edithe and her four orphaned sisters to make it alone in a child-reared family, one of 267,000 such family units in post-genocide Rwanda. But, by the time I met Edithe three years later, I saw little hint of a heavy heart. How had she come to lay down her personal burden? When Edithe shared her story with me and the secret of the joy she discovered in her young life, she made the way seem easy. "After months of feeling so alone with my burdens," she said, smiling, "I came to realize that every girl here carried something similar. I would never be able to come to know them, to listen to their stories or help bear their grief, if I continued to be closed in on myself, clinging ever so tightly to my pain only. In making room for others inside my heart, I found that my own pain began to fall away. Today, I love all these girls; they are a part of my life now. I am very happy. People ask me my secret and I tell them it is very simple. Let go of too much self-concern and make room for others. My life is full of loving and I have become light again. I hope I have made others happy, too." From the many girls with whom I saw Edithe interact, I feel confident that Edithe's hope has been realized. I, too, feel happier for the gift of meeting her.

Making Some Faith Connections

As I stand once again in the power of memory and reflection before the faces of Speciosa, Clebert, Edithe, and the slain children of Rwanda, I ponder anew the role each of us plays in the becoming of the other into whose face we gaze. From a faith perspective, we see in the face of another, especially the forgotten, neglected or abused, the face of the living God. Compassion does wear a human face. "What you do for the least of these, you do for me," Jesus insisted. The gospel of John theologizes about the responsibility love gives us for others, explaining that if we love, we live in God and God lives in us. Not only does God live in us, but if all who love live in God, then all live in us. The inclusion of everyone in us and in God flows from the conviction that there is no one in whom the spark of love can be entirely extinguished. If all live in us, then the only way to inner peace, as Speciosa realized, was to make peace with her enemies. For indeed, they were in her. They were her source of inner turmoil. And not only were these enemies in her, she herself was like them, was even one of them. She, too, recognized the power of hate in her own heart. But if hate was in her, so was the power of love, calling to her as God's selfless gift of compassion. It was a power that summoned her first in the silence of her own heart, but eventually in the face of those others from whom she had withheld her gaze.

The truth that the other is already in us is expressed poignantly in the Pauline doctrine of the Body of Christ.[7] Within our Christian faith story, the Risen Christ lives now as a many-membered body. No one is excluded from the growing womb of love. It groans as it grows to cosmic proportions beyond our human comprehension. We have been incorporated into this Body; what happens to any member of the body happens to the entire body. Nor can we say to another part of the body, we have no need of you. We all coexist, co-become. We live in and through the other. Such is a theological interpretation of the Body of Christ, the Pauline teaching that we are one though many. Only in and through the other can we hope to be the person we are intended to become, free and loving, mutually responsible to give and receive love. Young Edithe embodied this doctrine in her generous self-gift for the sake of others who needed her love and care. She made room in her poor, broken heart to receive others in their pain and, in the process, she herself was healed. Clebert, the prison guard, discovered this truth in the transformed lives of guilt-ridden

---

[7]The doctrine of the Body of Christ is brilliantly explored by Josiah Royce in his great sociological study, *The Problem of Christianity*, originally delivered as the Gifford Lectures of 1913. Royce argues that the genius of Paul the Apostle lay in his creating the powerful symbol of the Body of Christ to bring together the two great commandments of love of God and love of neighbor. These commandments had formerly stood side by side, but are now inseparably linked through Paul's writing, forming a new "third being." Paul called this "third being" a Mystery, a new way of loving, which encompasses love of God, love of each individual, and love for the whole Body or universal "beloved community." It is this third kind of loving, inseparable from the other two, to which the expanse of compassion reaches out.

and forlorn prisoners, uplifted by the power of mercy and forgiving love. As he beheld them first from afar, he began to let go of his personal claims to distance, innocence, and busyness.[8] Such distance had once enabled him to regard himself as a prison guard, not an inmate, separated out to look down on those others in their brokenness. His claim to innocence empowered him to judge self-righteously that he was not like them; and his incessant busyness, on the job and off, spared him any serious self-reflection in which his own past failings or inner yearnings might rise up. But as Clebert moved closer to face the other, those bringing forgiveness and those in need of it, he began to see himself in both groups. Gradually, Clebert faced his own vulnerable self—his own heart in need of healing. As he risked crossing over into others' lives, he found himself a transformed person, one who was discovering more about himself in the flawed but graced humanity of both prisoners and visitors. He saw each of them with new eyes—the eyes of compassionate love—the same gift he was being offered by them.

By the time I left Rwanda in mid-April 1994, I had achieved my sabbatical goal. I had met with and gathered hundreds of personal, communal, and ecclesial stories about people who had chosen forgiveness and reconciliation as a process, a way toward new life for them and their country; hatred and retaliation would only fuel more violence and ongoing hate. I might have left Rwanda content with this great gift. But God at work in the Rwandan people would not let me off the hook that easily. It was Sunday morning, March 19, the Feast of St. Joseph, our congregational patron and a special day for all Sisters of St. Joseph. We gathered at the Jesuit Center in Kigali for Eucharist with Les Bons Samaritains. Personal testimony is integral to their prayer

---

[8]I owe the call to overcome these three temptations (to claim innocence, distance, and busyness), as ways to heal our hardness of heart and learn vulnerability, to Emmanuel Katongole and Chris Rice in their work *Reconciling All Things* (Downers Grove, IL: Intervarsity Press, 2008).

together, and always follows the scripture readings. Anne Marie, the founder of Les Bons Samaritains, shared something of her incredible gratitude to God who had loved her and called her to form this group in the 1980s. At that time, years before the genocide, they had no way of imagining how their mission—to cross all borders bringing God's mercy and compassion to all, without exception—would one day serve as a powerful instrument of healing and forgiveness throughout their beloved but ravaged Rwanda. God was the very heart of who these Good Samaritans were, of that she was certain. Then Anne Marie called me to share a reflection with the people, but not until she had prefaced it with a huge challenge to me. I remember her words to me as I remember the biblical passage she shared: "Never forget what your own eyes have seen, nor let the memory of them fade from your heart. But teach them to your children and your children's children" (Deut 4:9). Then, Anne Marie added: "But, Cathy, when you go back to America, we don't want you to simply tell our stories. When you go back home, we want you to figure out where your divides are; cross over those borders and love there." Something about Anne Marie's challenge resounds in me like a bequest also. Similar to that of the slain children, I see in it a call to heal the past, to learn from it for the sake of a new, shared future, where all find a welcomed place. I've passed on this challenge to everyone, every group I meet, realizing that it was not intended for me alone. What are the divides that continue to create the illusion here in the United States that we are separate from one another, content to believe there is a "them" and an "us"? These are the borders we must be willing to cross if compassion is to forge the connection that makes us children of God and sisters and brothers to one another. How have class, race, religious or sexual identities, age, or abilities been used to oppress or marginalize whole groups of our sisters and brothers?[9]

---

[9]The Institute for Forgiveness and Reconciliation at Chestnut Hill College, which opened in 2008–9, is one concrete effort that has come of Anne Marie's

You've heard me say that I consider the Rwandan genocide survivors, who shared their broken hearts and transformed lives with me, to be my greatest teachers of compassion—but their lessons are not without their challenges. What needs to happen within my own heart for me to let go of any past grudge, any feeling of superiority, or judgment of others, all those self-deceptive blind spots that keep alive an illusion of separation? In confronting the horrors of what human beings do to one another, how do I resist the temptation to think that I am not like them? A young friend gave me a song shortly before I left for Rwanda and, even though there was no means of playing it while there, its melody and words were very present and at work in my heart. It's called the Compassion Song.[10]

Break my heart, O God, with what breaks your
     heart, O God.
Please break my heart.
Not that you need this invitation, not that you wait
     for my permission,
still this is my humble confession that I need so
     much more compassion.
Please, break my heart, O God, with what breaks
     your heart,
O God, Please break my heart.

As Christianity and so many world religions find life and our common future, sustained by the faith that all creation images in some way the divine life-giver, the people of

---

challenge. We seek to come together to face our divides and commit ourselves to doing the healing work that crosses over from exclusion to embrace, forging a new spirit of our shared humanity by repairing the past and lifting up what was oppressed. Only then can we assume our rightful place in a relationship of sisters and brothers, healed of all divisions. See our website at www.chc.edu/forgive.

[10]Jennifer Martin and Daughters of God, "Break My Heart: The Compassion Song," *Songs from the Heart* (Portland, OR: OCP Publications, 2002), no. 7.

Rwanda have made this faith sing and dance for me. As I have shared so often in story and in photos, you can't be in Rwanda and not dance. In the Rwandan people, I have seen the power of compassion come alive; the image of God present in radiant black faces that are grieving but graced. To be part of the Body of Christ with them gives me hope. We have every reason to dance!

The gospel question "Who is my neighbor?" with which the parable of the Good Samaritan opens, takes on global proportions today. We can no longer claim innocence, distance, or busyness to spare us from responsibility for the other into whose face we must gaze from every corner of our global home. With Jesus's words, "Go and do likewise," we face some level of responsibility for them all and they for us. *Ubuntu*—"I am because we are"—is the African proverb that expresses the reality for all of us theologically, sociologically, psychologically, and ethically. The people of Africa, Rwandans as my personal example, have much to teach us about the compassion connection that binds us all. *Ubuntu* is but another way of saying: There is no them; there's just us. And together, we are all one.

Conversation Starters

1. *Is there a lesson about compassion you relate to in any one of the stories recounted here? Why? Do you have a story of your own from which you've learned a compassion lesson?*
2. *Social media is a reality of our global experience today. Here in the West, we influence what others around our world see and hear. In what ways do you see social media as a force for good in our world? What concerns do you have about its negative influence?*
3. *Many people comfort themselves with the thought that something as horrific as the useless killing of so*

*many innocent people could never happen here. How
would you agree or disagree with such thinking?*

4. *How do you see forgiveness as a path to healing for
Rwanda and for us? Is there a social evil for which
we in the United States need to repent and ask forgiveness? How is forgiveness related to compassion?*

5

Learning Compassion from the "Small Heart" of Etty Hillesum

Recognizing the God of Compassion Wearing Our Human Face

God wants to come to us through people who come into our lives. This conviction is at the heart of incarnational faith. What a gift to have people whose way of living mirrors the God that we first met in the Hebrew scriptures, who took flesh in Jesus the Christ, indwelled the heart of that indiscriminately loving father, and that "good" Samaritan we met in Luke's gospel. When we encounter people who freely give of themselves without counting the cost, we might pause to ask, "Is this You, God, showing up here and now?" At least we can say, "God's got kin in them." But we need to slow down, pay attention or we might easily miss these love encounters—encounters that God desires for us even more than we may realize.

In my personal story I have found that the simple, ordinary life of my dad provides an alluring glimpse of God as freely given love. In the stories of the Rwandan people we see something of compassion's movement out of each person's self-enclosed life, with its unique pain and struggle, to connect with the lives of others, to carry their burdens, brokenness, and pain, allowing both giver and receiver to become more loving and whole in the process. From the ordinary, undramatic events that shaped the life of my father, to the outsized courage demonstrated by the broken-open hearts of Clebert, Speciosa, and Edithe, we learn that the circumstances of each life may look remarkably different, from the commonplace to the heroic, but the invitation to grow to one's own full stature as a compassion-bearer is the same for us all. Because both of these examples—the life of my big-hearted dad and the lives of so many open-hearted Rwandans—have been such a profound gift in my life, I share them with you. The work of making connections goes on in your heart, in your life, as it does in mine. Some days I'm better at making connections than others; I suspect it may be the same for you. Let's try to find some compassion threads and test them, because these stories are not finished until they intersect your story and those whom your story will touch. I believe that compassion is transmitted from one heart to another down through the ages—a part of the way Jesus continues to count on us.

Indeed, we go on giving life to others long after our earthly life is gone. I learned this lesson poignantly from reading the journals of a young Dutch Jew named Etty Hillesum, who died in Auschwitz in 1943.[1] There is so much more compassion alive in our world today because Etty lived than I can ever prove—but that this is so, I have no doubt. One of the ways that I feel called to make this more evident is by living the compassion that Etty has inspired and educed in me. After returning from Rwanda, I knew at a felt level that I left the

---

[1]Etty Hillesum, *An Interrupted Life and Letters from Westerbork* (New York: Henry Holt, 1996). This is the most popular and accessible edition of Etty's journals and letters. For my own study, I use the complete and unabridged publication titled *Etty: The Letters and Diaries of Etty Hillesum, 1941–1943*, ed. Klaas Smelik (Grand Rapids, MI: Eerdmans, 2002). This complete edition (800 pages) published by the Etty Hillesum Foundation contains almost double the diary entries (ten blue writing pad books; book no. 7 has never been found) and dozens of additional letters, including two that Etty sent describing her final departure from Westerbork. Direct quotes from Etty will appear with the page numbers from the complete text cited, unless the date of the journal entry is given.

geographical country behind me, but the beauty and pain, the forgiving love and challenge of its people lived on in me. Surely, I can say this of my father's life as well. It may seem more difficult to make the same claim about Etty Hillesum, whom I never met. How can this Dutch Jew, who died before I was born, go on living inside me also? Yet I feel no less certain that this is true. I sense the power of Etty's words and actions asking something of me. I pass her testimony on to you, as I reflect on this one, unlikely person, whose "small heart was chosen by God to bear so much" (514). This God of total, self-giving, irrepressible love for all is the One Etty came so close to resembling. At least that's the way I see her, how she has inspired me. Whether Etty is already a significant person to you or someone you are meeting for the first time, I invite you to open yourself to let her in. I promise you that God will slip in alongside her, because that's just the way it is. So let's make room. Once again, the Sufi poet Hafiz gives us reason to smile at just how much God desires to become one with us. Listen to his poem "No More Leaving":

> At some point
> Your relationship
> With God
> Will become like this:
> Next time you meet him in the forest
> or on a crowded city street
> There won't be anymore
> "Leaving."
> That is,
> God will climb into
> Your pocket.
> You will simply just take
> Yourself
> Along![2]

[2]Hafiz, "No More Leaving," in *The Gift: Poems by Hafiz, The Great Sufi Master*, trans. Daniel Ladinsky (London: Penguin Compass, 1999), 258.

The Metaphor of Making Room

The metaphor of making room is reminiscent of that capacity of the mother's womb to expand to hold more life. The *rechem* (womb-love) identity of God and all who share God's life is a most significant image to keep in mind as we learn about compassion from the heart of Etty Hillesum. With this image, I set out to talk about how the heart of Etty grew in S-I-Z-E[3] from that of a self-absorbed, young, Jewish, intellectual woman, living in Amsterdam in 1941, just a year after the Nazi takeover, to that of a totally other-centered, self-giving lover, who excluded no one from entry into her spacious, self-emptied heart. Though we know little of Etty's life before the war, what we do know through her journals and her letters abruptly ends with her departure for Auschwitz on September 7, 1943. Yet, I am confident that we have ample reason to describe Etty's heart as *rechem*. Yes, womb-love may be the best way to describe her that I can find.

Such a growth spurt of the heart in two short years seems highly unusual, that's true. Yet God can do incredible things in us, once that seed of God is given room to grow. I know no clearer proof of this than coming to know Etty Hillesum. In reading her journals, *An Interrupted Life,* one gets a precious look at her inner world, as it is exposed

---

[3]Bernard M. Loomer, "S-I-Z-E," *Criterion* 13, no. 3 (Spring 1974): 5–8. The metaphor of S-I-Z-E, abundantly present in Etty's own writing, is integral to the interwoven theological system of Bernard Loomer who describes "S-I-Z-E" (which always appears in this form in Loomer's works) this way: "By S-I-Z-E I mean the stature of [your] soul, the range and depth of [your] love, [your] capacity for relationships. I mean the volume of life you can take into your being and still maintain your integrity and individuality, the intensity and variety of outlook you can entertain in the unity of your being without feeling defensive or insecure. I mean the strength of your spirit to encourage others to become freer in the development of their diversity and uniqueness. I mean the power to sustain more complex and enriching tensions. I mean the magnanimity of concern to provide conditions that enable others to increase in stature." Ibid., 6.

for consideration, interrogation. I offer you excerpts from Etty's journals and letters, certainly a limited and partial perspective, but one that I find suggestive of how God's unconditional love and compassion grew to such immense proportions within her, transforming her first into a "girl who learned to kneel" (60–61) and then into one who "broke her body as bread because people were hungry and had gone without for so long" (230).

People have debated whether Etty fits the characteristics of a mystic.[4] I have absolutely no hesitation in affirming Etty's mystical encounters with God, the God she found both within her, and also living and dying, suffering and rising in the concrete, historical situation of the Holocaust in which Etty lived her wild yet precious life. What is it in me that draws me to Etty? Why do I want so much for you to meet her? What does Etty want to do in you? With these questions I begin this exploration, realizing that for you, as reader, the third is the most significant and the other two may become your questions as well.

One of the characteristics of a spiritual or mystical text is its capacity to evoke an embodied, value-laden response in its readers.[5] In the designation "mystical," I intend the definition offered by David Steindl-Rast, OSB, as "an experience of universal belonging."[6] That experience is available to all of us, because the ultimate gift of compassion, as unre-

---

[4]At the centenary celebration of Etty's birth, held at the University of Ghent in January of 2014, I offered a paper on Etty, interpreting her writings as a spiritual text, often with mystical perspectives to share. Present at the conference were other scholars who cautioned those who would limit the value of the multiple meanings emerging from Etty's writings or reduce the complexity of this heroic woman's life and words to a solely "religious" significance alone. I totally agree that Etty Hillesum exists for the world, believer and nonbeliever alike.

[5]I read and reread *An Interrupted Life* as a spiritual/mystical text, realizing that others interpret it primarily as a historical document, a psychological study of a young, erotic, impressionable woman, an early feminist, or as a cherished memoir of Holocaust literature. All are appropriate, none exclusive.

[6]David Steindl-Rast, OSB, quoted in "The Monk and the Rabbi: Mysticism and the Peak Experience." Dialogue between Brother David Steindl-Rast and Rabbi Lawrence Kushner (www.youtube.com, A Network for Grateful Living, May 2009).

stricted love for all, knows no boundaries. Each of us must attend to fragmentary moments holding out this experience for us. This broader meaning of a mystic is urgently needed today. Karl Rahner, SJ, esteemed by many as the greatest Catholic theologian of the twentieth century, wrote that "the Christian of the future will be a mystic or will fail to exist at all."[7] I concur with Rahner, who explains mysticism as "a genuine experience of God emerging from the very heart of our existence."[8] This entire book is grounded in the conviction of each one's personal experience of God as compassion, intended for all. In reading Etty's diary entries, I find not only beautiful and profoundly intimate descriptions of the God who found her, but, like Ignatius of Loyola, Etty has left the rest of us who are still searching for more of God, more of Love, some clear guidelines to follow.

Clearing Out Our Heart's Clutter

I was first drawn to Etty's description of meditation and her decision to practice it because it reminded me of a teaching from St. John of the Cross: "God will take up as much room in our hearts as we are willing to give over."[9] Prayer is simply the act of making ourselves available to the Divine who is always coming. Within a few short months of journal keeping, Etty shared her resolve:

I'll "turn inward" for half an hour each morning before work, and listen to my inner voice. . . . But it's not so simple, that sort of "quiet hour." It has to be learned. A lot of unimportant inner litter and bits and pieces

---

[7]Karl Rahner, SJ, *Theological Investigations VI*, 149.

[8]Ibid.

[9]See Iain Matthew, *The Impact of God: Soundings from St. John of the Cross* (London: Hodder and Stoughton, 1995). See chapter 6, "The Right Kind of Emptiness," in which Matthew breaks open meanings from John of the Cross's *Living Flame of Love*, inviting us to get out of the way in order to give the ever approaching God room to maneuver.

have to be swept out first. . . . True, there may be edifying emotions and thoughts, too, but the clutter is ever present. So let this be the aim of the meditation: to turn one's innermost being into a vast empty plain, with none of that treacherous undergrowth to impede the view. So that something of "God" can enter you, and something of "Love," too. Not the kind of love-de-luxe that you revel in deliciously for half an hour, taking pride in how sublime you can feel, but the love you can apply to small, everyday things. (June 8 [1941], Sunday morning, 9.30)

From early on in Etty's spiritual journey, she grasped the essential need for the concrete over the abstract, for a love that was made visible in deeds, rather than in lofty feelings or "delicious revelings." Etty understood spiritual growth as a capacity to make room—clearing out the inner litter and ever-present clutter—the "treacherous undergrowth" that impeded her view of a larger life and a greater love. She wanted to make room inside her for something of God and Love to enter and take up their dwelling. Having already made the claim that God often chooses to come to us through other people, who reflect for us a life of immense, spacious loving, there was for young Etty such a person. His name was Julius Spier, "a Jungian psychoanalyst cum palm reader and spiritual guru,"[10] who over time, Etty claimed, "dug God out of her."[11] It seems clear from Etty's journals that no one played a more significant role in Etty's spiritual development than Julius Spier, as complex and multifaceted as their relationship was. "S," as she referred to him most frequently, served as Etty's therapist, she, as his secretary.

---

[10]From the foreword by Eva Hoffman, in *Etty Hillesum: An Interupted Life and Letters from Westerbork* (New York: Henry Holt, 1996), ix.

[11]From a letter of Etty to her close friend, Tide. Etty explained that this work of digging up God in her had really been done by Spier, but Etty made herself available, open and receptive to this inner work recommended by him (Letter to Tide, September 11, 1942, p. 567).

But he became her trusted confidant, her intellectual peer, and, for a brief time, her lover. Even in her early experience of Spier, Etty remarked that it was more his "way of living" that influenced her than any words he spoke, as dedicated as she was to writing so many of them down. In Spier's behavior, she witnessed "a heart open to a multitude" (59). This openness to others, Etty realized, was dependent on the amount of room she gave to God inside her. She set her heart to that ongoing task of carving out space. In fact, Etty became clearer and clearer that this inner work was what she must focus on. On August 26, 1941, she wrote: "There is a really deep well inside me. And in it dwells God. Sometimes I am there, too. But more often stones and grit block the well, and God is buried beneath. Then He must be dug out again" (91).

Little by little Etty gave herself over to this inner work of letting God find more room inside her, a space she knew to be often confused and riddled by ambivalent feelings. I know I can so easily identify with the blocks Etty identified within her, those which held her back from giving herself away in love. She realized that "personal pettinesses" erected a "barricade" in her, thus limiting the volume of life she could take in. "And you must go on finding a way through all the pettinesses—of which you are chock-full and of which you cannot honestly imagine you will ever be rid—if you are to understand anything about life and human beings" (176). Etty's willingness to embrace this process with all the work it entailed may well set her apart from many of us who give up when change is not immediate and spiritual progress less than straightforward. If the range and depth of Etty's love were to grow, her petty vanities needed to diminish.

> I am still assailed far too much by words like these. I prayed early this morning, "Lord, free me from all these petty vanities. They take up too much of my inner life, and I know only too well that other things matter

much more than being thought nice and charming by one's fellows." (335)

Growing through Struggle: The Lesson Repeats Itself

These hints of the struggle are surely one of the great contributions Etty made to helping all humankind "increase in stature," as Bernard Loomer suggests. But these inner/outer conflicts would eventually serve as the "very real stuff" through which Etty grew toward a great-hearted being. She more and more came to depend on the God who was so close, right there inside her, one with whom she held intimate conversations. Yes, Etty believed firmly that she had room for it all because God was becoming more and more important all the time. She speaks directly to God, her inner center, and says confidently: "I think I work well with You, God, that we work well together. I have assigned an ever larger dwelling space to You, and I am also beginning to become faithful to You. . . .The powerful center spreads its rays to the outermost boundaries" (223).

A God outside of human history cannot do justice to God or to history. Etty Hillesum understood these connections intuitively, and they grew exponentially as she refused to escape or deny the reality in which her lot was cast. On July 7, 1942, at 8:00 pm, Etty recorded her day's reflections:

Everything has simply fallen away from me, leaving no trace, and I feel more receptive than ever before. Next week no doubt it will be the turn of the Dutch Jews. With each minute that passes I shed more wishes and desires and attachments. I am ready for everything, for anywhere on this earth, wherever God may send me, and I am ready to bear witness in any situation and unto death that life is beautiful and meaningful and that it is not God's fault that things are as they are at present, but our own. . . . There are moments when I can see right through life and the human heart, when I understand more and more and become calmer and calmer and am filled with a faith in God that has grown so quickly inside me that it frightened me at first but has now become inseparable from me. (480–81)

By the time Etty's most cherished friend Julius Spier died in September of 1942, her attachment to him had fallen away as well, and she was receptive even to life without him. Gratitude became the distinguishing characteristic of the life she so fully embraced. On the day of Spier's death, September 5, 1942, it was her deepest emotion.

I now realize, God, how much You have given me. So much that was beautiful and so much that was hard to bear. Yet whenever I showed myself ready to bear it, the hard was directly transformed into the beautiful. And the beautiful was sometimes much harder to bear, so overpowering did it seem. To think that one small human heart can experience so much, oh God, so much suffering and so much love, I am so grateful to You, God, for having chosen my heart, in these times, to experience all the things it has experienced. (514)

Rather than being paralyzed by the loss of her beloved friend, Etty expressed deep, inner freedom—much of which she credited to the gift of their mutual love, which had everything to do with the love of God in her.

What energies I possess have been set free inside me. You taught me to speak the name of God without embarrassment. You were the mediator between God and me, and now you, the mediator, have gone, and my path leads straight to God. It is right that it should be so. And I shall be the mediator for any other soul I can reach. (516)

What Spier had done for her, Etty must be available to do for others. To be a mediator between God and other human beings—is this not what each of us has been created to be, as unique reflections of the God in whose image we are created; the God whose seed grows inside us? Etty took on this compassion-bearing role to help others see more of God and love still present in their everyday lives, despite the destructive forces closing in on them. Not only did Etty share the way she saw these times and what they asked of good people, but she longed to take care of those she loved, and others she did not.

> I am so grateful for this life. I feel I am growing, I am aware of my faults and my pettinesses each new day, but I also know my potential. And I have so much love; I love a few good friends, but that love is not a fence erected against others; my love is far-flung, all-embracing and broad enough to include very many of whom I am really not all that fond. (254)

Without using the word compassion explicitly, Etty's description of the kind of love she bears, a love that is far-flung and all-embracing certainly fits a *rechem* heart. Somehow all persons must be embraced in that single love. At least that must be the direction our love takes. In Etty's words, "When love for all mankind is not involved in some way or another, we eventually become impoverished and limited" (302). The lack of love for all, beginning with the person next to us, is the reason for all disasters in our world, as Etty reasoned:

> All disasters stem from us. Why is there a war? Perhaps because now and then I might be inclined to snap at my neighbor. Because I and my neighbor and everyone else do not have enough love. Yet we could fight war . . . by releasing, each day, the love that is shackled inside us and giving it a chance to live. (307)

Life's most horrific of ambiguities found room in Etty's large heart, because she resolved to "try to face up to Your world, God, not to escape from reality into beautiful dreams—though I believe that beautiful dreams can exist beside the most horrible reality" (384). Without ever blinding herself to the mounting suffering of people around her, Etty acknowledged at the same time a deep sense of oneness large enough to embrace the whole nation of humankind. This she saw as part of her work:

> One must live with oneself as if one lived with a whole nation of people. And in oneself one then comes to recognize all the good and bad qualities of mankind. And if one wants to forgive others, one must first learn to forgive one's own bad qualities. That is probably the hardest thing a person can learn. . . . Which means accepting above all, and magnanimously, that one does make mistakes and does have lapses. (Tuesday, September 22, 1942).

Compassion's Gift Intended for Oneself—No Exceptions

How helpful it is in learning the compassion of God to learn compassion for oneself, whom God loves so tenderly! Pausing to test this claim in your own experience seems an important exercise. Let God hold you long enough to assure you that Compassion loves you without limits or conditions—just as you are. Let God remind you to love yourself with that same compassion born in you of God. Etty found great inner peace in this assurance. It is available to all of us. Etty acknowledged that a growing amount of inner freedom is demanded to stay at one's post, as she often called it. She yearned to see life and each person for who they really are and not try to control or change anything into her own preferred image.

We help to create each other, sharing as we do in that divine work. Etty's concern for others was vast, including a Gestapo soldier who yelled at her. Her love for each individual as a real person and not an abstraction became the building blocks for her slow process of transformation into a woman of such notable S-I-Z-E. In each person, she found a human being, more like herself than different, one in whom the image of God longed to take on a unique contour, a human face. Thus, she could write:

> I am not easily frightened. Not because I am brave, but because I know that I am dealing with human beings and that I must try as hard as I can to understand everything that anyone ever does. And that was the real import of this morning: not that a disgruntled young Gestapo officer yelled at me, but that I felt no indignation, rather a real compassion. . . . Yes, he looked harassed and driven, sullen and weak. . . . What needs eradicating is the evil in man, not man himself. (259)

A short unexpected conversation with Jan Bool, a close but stubborn friend, waiting at the tram stop, offers another good example of Etty's connection with every human being. In each, she saw a part of herself.

> "What is it in human beings that makes them want to destroy others?" Jan asked bitterly. I said, "Human beings, you say, but remember that you're one yourself." And strangely enough he seemed to acquiesce, grumpy, gruff old Jan. "The rottenness of others is in us, too," I continued to preach at him. "I see no other solution, I really see no other solution than to turn inward and to root out all the rottenness there. . . ." And Jan, who so unexpectedly agreed with everything I said, was approachable and interested and no longer proffered any of his hard-boiled social theories. Instead he said, "Yes, it's too easy to turn your hatred loose on the outside, to live for nothing but the moment of revenge. We must try to do without that." (245)

Life in the "Belly of Paradox" Again

As I savor the writings of Etty Hillesum, I am drawn to reflect on the paradox of her life. As a young woman who aborted her own natural child, Etty gave birth willingly and painfully to so many, bearing them within her in love until they flourished. Herein lies the mystery of one growing in the likeness of God. The image of life-bearer is so indubitably clear. "To carry the other with one, always and everywhere, and to live with him there. . . . And not just with one, but with many. To draw the other into one's inner space and to assign him a place where he can grow and unfold. . . . It makes for great responsibility" (281).

In opening up to carry others within her, Etty realized that there grew inside her a great tenderness. Certainly, this was a certain sign that God dwelled there—the God of tenderness and compassion, growing ever larger.

> One must divide one's single great tenderness into a thousand small tendernesses, lest one succumbs to the weight of that one great tenderness. A thousand small tendernesses: for a dog in the road, or for an old flower seller—and finding the right word for someone in need. And also not feeling sad because one imagines one cannot express that single, great, strong feeling one carries inside. . . . One must also be able to wear and to bear, to tolerate and endure, one's own strong feelings . . . not just for one man but for so many of God's creatures which also have a right to our attention and love. (348–49)

To experience the compassion connection as the tenderness we feel and show to life in all its forms, from a dog on the road to a stranger in need. Is this not a longing in each of us: to give and receive tenderness in a world too often cruel? Etty's tenderness led her to make this request of God—to take on herself the mind and heart of the entire barracks, the entire concentration camp.

> At night, as I lay in the camp on my plank bed, surrounded by women and girls, quietly sobbing and tossing and turning, women and girls who often told me during the day, "We don't want to think, we don't want to feel, otherwise we are sure to go out of our minds," I was sometimes filled with an infinite tenderness, and lay awake for hours . . . and I prayed, "Let me be the thinking heart of these barracks." And that is what I want to be again. The thinking heart of a whole concentration camp. (542–43)

Etty's care for others extended far beyond the concentration camp itself. She longed to have a voice in healing the wounds that divided the whole human family—all God's "warring creatures." She felt deep inside her the pain of every division.

> With a sharp pang, all of suffering mankind's nocturnal distress and loneliness passes now through my small heart. . . . One day, I would love to travel through all the world, oh God; I feel drawn right across all frontiers and feel a bond with all Your warring creatures. And I would like to proclaim that bond in a small, still voice but also compellingly and without pause. But first I must be present on every battlefront and at the center of all human suffering. Then I will surely have the right to speak out. (531)

The God Who Found Room in Etty's Heart

A year and a half after Etty resolved to turn inward every morning in hopes of clearing out the "treacherous overgrowth" that obstructed her view of the world, her inner space seemed ever more open to take it all in. Etty's capacity to hold so much within her and to pour it out in love was clearly the work of God in her. This outpoured love would help to build a new world. She credited her vision and endurance to her steady, ever-present, and intimate relationship with her God. "What a strange story it really is, my story: the girl who could not kneel. Or its variation: the girl who learned to pray. That is my most intimate gesture, more intimate even than being with a man. After all, one can't pour the whole of one's love out over a single man, can one?" (547).

To play a part in building the new world that Etty already saw and experienced growing within her—for this, Etty prayed. More than once, she asked that she might live a long time. On July 3, 1942, she tempered her request:

> If I am not granted that wish, well, then somebody else will perhaps do it, carry on from where my life has been cut short. And that is why I must try to live a good and faithful life to my last breath: so that those who come after me do not have to start all over again, need not face the same difficulties. Isn't that doing something for future generations? (461–62)

The vastness of Etty's *rechem* heart extended beyond the suffering world on which her love was poured. It included her care for the generations to follow—that they might not have to start from scratch, learning how to love boundlessly. She longed to "mirror God's image full size" as her favorite poet, Rilke, prayed.[12] God was counting on her, and Etty was up to the task. As she grew more and more in that likeness of God, her will seemed more closely united with that of the God within her. Like Jesus, the Beloved of God, Etty knew she must be willing to suffer because of the

---

[12]Rainer Maria Rilke, *Rilke's Book of Hours: Love Poems to God*, trans. Anita Barrows and Joanna Macy (New York: Riverhead Books, 1996), 59.

ambiguous presence of evil, as well as good, in this world that God so loves. How real was Etty's awareness of the cost: how relentless her willingness to endure it. This did not mean that Etty did not experience weakness and trepidation, but her faith never wavered. Her inner strength grew in direct proportion to her awareness of her need. Late in the evening of July 20, 1942, Etty expressed in her journal her prayer of that morning:

> Oh God, times are too hard for frail people like myself. I know that a new and kinder day will come. . . . And there is only one way of preparing for the new age, by living it even now in our hearts. . . . I feel responsible for that great and beautiful feeling for life I carry within me, and I must try to shepherd it safe and sound through these times, towards better ones. (498)

The force of love in her, Etty believed, was so elemental that it would and could build a whole new world. To this fundamental truth, she prayed to be faithful to the end, so that she and her people might be worthy to have a say in building a new world.

> Against every new outrage and every fresh horror, we shall put up one more piece of love and goodness, drawing strength from within ourselves. . . . And if we should survive unhurt in body and soul, but above all in soul, without bitterness and without hatred, then we shall have a right to a say after the war. Maybe I am an ambitious woman: I would like to have just a tiny little bit of a say. (615)

Etty's Final Journey to Westerbork and Auschwitz

By the time Etty arrived to stay in Westerbork, the detention center before the final transport to the death camps of

Auschwitz, she was asking for the right to have "a tiny, little bit of a say" in shaping the new world that she believed mightily "God so loved" (Jn 3:16). Into that world, John's gospel tells us, that the "Word" became flesh in Jesus—a brother Jew, like Etty and her millions of suffering sisters and brothers. If love was able to have the final word in them, Etty believed, they too would have "a right to a say after the war." A close resemblance to God's Word once again took human flesh in this young Jewish woman, a resemblance too undeniable not to acknowledge.

We know nothing of the final months of Etty's life, those she endured between September 7 and November 30, 1943, when her death at Auschwitz was recorded. From my own personal relationship with Etty, I feel confident that by the time Etty faced her death, her *rechem* heart could not be dwarfed even as she confronted the most abominable end. Though we know nothing of the details, Etty did not go to her death alone. God had long ago slipped into Etty's pocket; there would be no more leaving. She had earlier asked: "At difficult moments like these, I often wonder what You intend with me, oh God, and therefore what I intend with You" (520). This wonderment was answered ultimately for both God and Etty in a precise way, unknown to us. Etty often intimated that this most intimate of all relationships, the one between herself and God, needed to be consummated in sacred privacy. Before its mystery, words cease and silence prevails. At that final moment, Etty's heart, the one she and her God shared, broke open and tender compassion was released. Of this I am certain, because in coming to love Etty, it has reached me.

That truth and a final image she offered of a spider web provide a compassion connection for us, as well. To find ourselves in an inseparable bond with Etty Hillesum, who has gone before us, invites us to hold on to the thread she has spun and thrown ahead for us to grasp. We reach for it, as she weaves this metaphor:

I shall try to convey to you how I feel, but am not sure if my metaphor is right. When a spider spins its web, does it not cast the main threads ahead of itself; and then follow along them from behind? The main path of my life stretches like a long journey before me and already reaches into another world. . . . Life here hardly touches my deepest resources—physically, perhaps, you do decline a little, and sometimes you are infinitely sad—but fundamentally you keep growing stronger. I just hope that it can be the same for you and all my friends. We need it, for we still have so much to experience together and so much work to do. And so I call upon you: stay at your inner post, and please do not feel sorry or sad for me, there is no reason to. (616–17)[13]

To stay at our inner post until we, too, grow to full stature and do our part in shaping that new world for which Etty gave her one beautiful life, her one small, chosen heart. We now ask to mirror, full-size, the God into whose image Etty had surely grown.

Conversation Starters

1. *Once again this chapter offers examples of loss that paradoxically are the means of new discoveries about oneself, others, and our world. Find some sections of Etty's journal entries that share this lesson. How*

---

[13]Etty sent this letter to her close friends Jopie and Klaas Smelik, whose nephew ultimately saw to the publication of Etty's writings some thirty years later. Dr. Klaas Smelik today directs the Etty Hillesum Foundation at the University of Ghent in Belgium. Though addressed to a few close friends, these pleading words from Etty are extended to all of us who are able to hear. Etty had asked to have a small say in building a new world. "Stay at your inner post," she urges, there is still so much work to be done. A new, compassionate world needs to grow from our spacious inner life.

have you learned from an experience of loss that has made you stronger?

2. What do you hear from Etty that connects you with a larger purpose for your own life?

3. How does what's happening inside us influence how we respond to things happening around us? Can you give an example from your own experience?

COMPASSION AS THE SPIRALING ENERGY OF THE CHURCH'S COMMUNION

How Might Our Church Resemble More Closely the Triune Heart of God?

6

Vatican II Reclaims Church as Communion

In the Image of our Triune God

A Church That Must Die to Itself

If you've been paying attention to how this compassion connection is threaded, you may have noticed that there's quite a bit of letting go and loss involved in becoming who we are, as reflections of the God who is self-giving love for all. That same paradox of losing in order to find, dying in order to live, will continue in Part III with its focus on the church. As I consider the role of the church in the world today, I find Etty Hillesum to be a good example. Not because Etty was a Jew and unchurched, but because Etty lived a compassionate life inside and out. Her lived experience reveals not only an immense love poured out into the world, but also a capacity to carry the world and all its people, the nasty Gestapo soldier and her beloved Spier, tenderly within her. I propose that a similar awareness provides the most appropriate way to engage this entire section on the church emerging from Vatican II. We are called to draw the church inside our own heart, make room for it there in all its complexity, and from there look out on the church's life and mission in the world.

The question of the church's role in our troubled world is never far from my mind and heart. My life in the church has caused me inner turmoil and deep lament, while overwhelming me also with profound grace and immense gratitude. The best way I can explain that grace is to say that I have come to know at an experiential level, that the church is in me, just as surely as I am in the church. I believe that God has offered me this grace and extends it to you, those of you who share the Christian vocation with me. We know that to bear life within one's own body is the role of a mother. Many of you know firsthand that mothering brings with it life's greatest joys, but also can be the source of its greatest pain. It was an intimate experience of my own mother that prepared me for this surprising understanding of my relationship with the church. It happened like this.

Before her death, my mother contracted a flesh-eating bacterium that left her body weak and fragile, broken open with eight gaping wounds, which even after surgery required the most intensive and specialized care. This included her need to lie on a bed of hot sand, which offered the only hope of healing her wounds from the inside out. There, she lay in a morphine-induced, semi-coma for 104 days. This graced but painful time for us, her five children, found us gathered in shifts around her hospital bed, day and night. I'm sure many of you have had similar experiences around the bedside of a dying loved one; perhaps your own mother—a sacred place, yielding profound lessons, seldom learned in any other way. One lesson, particularly meant for me, returns again today.

Gazing day after day on my mother's broken open, frail body, I became intensely aware that I had lived inside that body; this body, so weak and needy, was my first home. Everything I needed to come to life, her body provided. The very thought overwhelmed me with love and gratitude. I loved this body, now, in its brokenness, more than ever.

A few short weeks after my mother's death, while on a

directed retreat, I had a prayer experience, during which I began to weep with that same image of my mother's broken body. But, as I told my retreat director, I knew almost immediately that I wasn't weeping for my mother. This powerful image was about the church. I will never doubt that Mary, Mother of the Church, speaks to us still in the silence, since I knew then and I know now, beyond a shadow of doubt, that my mother spoke these words to me. Was it my mom or our mother, Mary—it hardly matters—the words were clear: "Cathy, can you love this Church, which once also gave you life, but which now is broken and dying of some flesh-eating wounds? Can you love it the same way you love me?" I know my tears that day were tears of compassion and a willingness to say "YES." I will not run away or abandon this body, the church, which mothered me in faith and now needs my mothering—our mothering. And so again today, I hear a compassion plea ringing out: that the church, as Christ's Body, might become purified from the inside out—healed of its arrogance, its need for power and control, its greed and protective cover-ups—relieved of all its inner clutter, in order to become less "stubborn sod" and more "transparent pool—reflecting God, only God." Praying with these words from a favorite poem, titled "The Pool of God" by the Carmelite nun, Jessica Powers, invites me to plead with Mary that the church might come a little more closely to resemble her.

> There was nothing in the Virgin's soul that belonged
>   to the Virgin—
> no word, no thought, no image, no intent.
> She was a pure, transparent pool reflecting God,
>   only God . . .
>
> God was her sky and she who mirrored Him
> became His firmament . . .
> And when I gaze into her selfless depths

an anguish in me grows
to hold such blueness and to hold such fire.

I pray to hollow out my earth and be
filled with these waters of transparency.
I think that one could die of this desire,
seeing oneself dry earth or stubborn sod.
Oh, to become a pure pool like the Virgin,
water that lost the semblance of water
and was a sky like God.[1]

To see the church, and myself as part of it, hollowed out is
a bold prayer. I pray with Mary and my own mother for the
desire to let this prayer be done in me and in our church.
Our world so needs the outpoured love and goodness our
God longs to share with all—no withholding. Christ longs
to find in his church a wide-open, broken heart that "holds
both sinner and saint close to its bosom."[2]

This conviction that the church is in me as well as my
being in the church is supported by the telling words of Etty
Hillesum once again. When her grumpy friend Jan Bool
questioned the rotten things human beings were doing to
one another, Etty asked Jan if he were not a human being
too. Was not the same rottenness in him that he saw in
others? The only solution to overcoming evil in our world
is to root it out in ourselves. Hmm. . . . And so I've come
to claim traces of arrogance, self-protection, a need to
control in my own heart and beg to become more humble
and self-aware, as I dare to call the church to account.[3] The

---

[1] Jessica Powers, "The Pool of God," in *The Selected Poetry of Jessica Powers*,
ed. Regina Siegfried and Robert Morneau (Washington, DC: ICS Publications,
1999), 63.

[2] *Lumen Gentium*, the Dogmatic Constitution on the Church, a principal
document of the Second Vatican Council (1964), 8 (www.vatican.va).

[3] For further insight on this concept of "humble blaming," see Lewis Smedes,
The Art of Forgiving, where he names "humble blaming" as the only authentic

love with which I want the church to repent and heal is the same love a mother has for her imperfect, sometimes sinful children, the *rechem* heart of the prodigal son's father. My longing for the church to beat with the heart of that Good Samaritan asks me also to help lift up the church, fallen among robbers and lying by the side of the road. Are not both the healer and the wounded in me as well?

I am very much indebted to my spiritual mentor, Karl Rahner, SJ, whose theology of the church has more than a little influenced and inspired me. I picture myself still sitting at his feet, listening to his great intellect and experiencing his pastoral heart. Of course, like Etty Hillesum, I never met Karl Rahner, who nonetheless lives on in me.[4] One of the things I respect most about Rahner was his willingness to criticize the church, and do so boldly, because he loved it so much. As early as the 1940s Rahner wrote about the sinful church. He refused to believe that there were two churches, with people in it who sinned, while the church *as such* remained unsullied. No, we are a holy but sinful church, Rahner insisted. His own student, Johann Baptist Metz, put it this way: "Rahner has the church in his guts, so he feels its failures like indigestion."[5]

---

kind of practice. We call another to face responsibility for wrongdoing, while acknowledging that we ourselves might be the next one to fall.

[4]I want to express my gratitude to Leo O'Donovan, SJ, a renowned Rahner scholar, for deepening this conviction in me. In 2004, to celebrate the centenary of Karl Rahner's birth, Father O'Donovan, a former student of Rahner's, and I, who never met the man, co-directed a weekend seminar entitled "Rahner: The Man and His Meaning," in which I made this claim of seeing myself as Rahner's "spiritual daughter." How empowered and grateful I continue to be in the strong affirmation of Leo O' Donovan that it was clear to him in listening to me that this relationship was real.

[5]Johann Baptist Metz, "Do We Miss Karl Rahner?" in *A Passion for God: The Mystical-Political Dimension of Christianity* (Mahwah, NJ: Paulist Press, 1998), 99. What troubled Rahner most about the church was its forgetfulness of its own provisionality—by replacing the liberating Mystery of God with itself. What I find so telling in this quote about Rahner is its close resemblance to the *rechem* womb-love we've identified as God's very life force. The church is held in Rahner's *splanknizoimai* (entrails or guts) used in Greek to mean compassion. For

I acknowledge that the church has caused me much grief, but it is a heaviness I am not willing to put down. I will carry it until it is transformed into life, and the burden becomes light.

With Oscar Romero and so many witnesses to enduring love for the church, I do not believe in death without resurrection. Certain institutional structures and historical forms of the church must die for the sake of new life. The prophetic and mystical Guatemalan poet in exile, Julia Esquivel says this:

> I am no longer afraid of death. I know well its dark, cold corridors leading to life. I am afraid, rather, of that life which does not come out of death. . . . I am afraid of my own fear and even more the fear of others, who do not know where they are going, who continue clinging to what they think is life, which we know to be death. . . . I live each day to kill death and I die each day to give birth to life.[6]

The willingness to let go, to die in order to live, repeats itself as one of compassion's greatest lessons. The church must continuously be a student in the school of compassion. We have but one Teacher, Jesus reminded us (Mt 23). Birthing a church resembling God's own Heart of Compassion is the work of God, who is Spirit, but Jesus is counting on us. It will take each and all of us to do our part to help unclutter the church's heart, to free it to become more effectively the presence and action of God's compassion in and for our aching world.

---

me, Rahner speaks from that place of God in him. For more on Rahner and his love for the church he criticizes, see the work of another Rahner student, Harvey D. Egan, SJ, *Karl Rahner: Mystic of Everyday Life* (New York: Crossroad, 1998).

[6]Julia Esquivel, "I Am Not Afraid of Death," in *Threatened with Resurrection: Prayers and Poems from an Exiled Guatemalan* (Elgin, IL: Brethren Press, 1994), 67.

Communion in the Energy of Compassion

Already as I begin to reflect on the call of the church to draw all into a communion in compassion, I both see the compassionate face of Pope Francis in his continuous outreach to the lost and broken people of our world and hear his challenging pleas to the church, especially in its episcopal leadership, to let go of all privileged positions, to break down confining walls of separation, and go out to the margins of society where the gospel message belongs. Have you not felt in Pope Francis this outpoured love for all—no withholding—and his insistence that this is the mission entrusted to us all?

In the chapters that follow, I hope to tap into some of the dynamic energy available to the church to become more authentically who it is: an energy for new life that continues to flow from the Heart of God and the sustaining grace of the Second Vatican Council. Yes, more than fifty years after the council, the Spirit yearns to draw the church deeper into God's triune life, the Womb of compassion that is our Creator God, the Heart of compassion embodied in Jesus, and the Vessel of compassion poured out in the Spirit. If the church is to grow into this triune image of the God it reflects, it is imperative that all who claim to be a part of this gathered people discover anew what this means. How are we to participate in growing this Body to full stature— mirroring this God full-size? This is our life's quest: to give and receive glimpses, at least, of the inexhaustible Mystery of God's compassion for all. Otherwise, I can see no reason for a church to exist. Do you know people, as I do, who have already reached this conclusion that the church has no purpose? Yet I believe that the documents and spirit of Vatican II hold untapped energy to reform and empower the church today. But we must help free that Spirit of life.

Emerging clearly from the documents of Vatican Council II, particularly its Dogmatic Constitution on the Church, *Lumen Gentium*, the post–Vatican II church is best understood as a sacrament of humanity's "communion in God's own life," to be poured out in love "for the salvation of the whole world" (*LG*, 1). I think it important to note from the beginning that the church is a sign or sacrament of *humanity*'s communion in God's own life. In fact, all of life is a co-sharer in this same communion life. The church is simply a sign, a wake-up call, more or less credible, of what God is doing, how Love is unfolding in and beyond history, in infinitely diverse manifestations.

The Spiraling Dynamics of Communion to Be Distinguished but Not Separated

Each of the remaining chapters within this section will describe communion as a spiraling dynamic energy, a mutual interplay, sometimes referred to as "a divine dance."[7] These four chapters need to be understood as a whole. Each plays an essential role in the church's growth into the image of God's compassion. You may more easily identify one as your preference or your strength, but I invite you to open yourself to understand the need for all four dimensions of communion to mutually interact, if each person within the One Body and the body as a whole, living organism is to grow. With confidence, we can be sure that the inexhaustible Mystery of God has more to teach us, more grace with which to flood our lives.

Whatever your relationship with the church as a social body presently is, ask yourself if there was ever a time in your life when the church provided a sacred space where the divine broke through, whether through an experience of a particular liturgy, a sacrament, a special retreat or prayer

---

[7]Richard Rohr with Mike Morrell, The Divine Dance: The Trinity and Your Transformation (London: SPCK, 2016), 69.

experience, or by providing a place of quiet and solitude where God could find you? Where or how has the church been a means through which the Divine has broken into your ordinary, human life with a Presence or Power too clear to deny, either in good times or in bad? If the church has not been your primary vehicle for accessing your own spiritual life, do you know people you admire for whom it has been this?

In my own life, it is clear to me that the church has been a living reality, a community of people, faithful and flawed, through whom a holy meeting has taken place. A personal relationship between me and God has been formed and nurtured. God has claimed me, loved me and invited me to say "YES" to God's self-gift of grace, because of the church. The church has led me to Jesus, who reveals to me the Face of God, in whose image we are all created as sisters and brothers.

I hope that you too, upon reflection, have discovered that God and you live in communion—God lives in you and you in God. That's simply the way it is. To make communion in God and with all others real in our world is to become compassionate to the extent possible for us at this time in our salvation history. The circle of divine communion excludes no one. The poet Rilke offers these words to echo God's desire: "Go to the limits of your longing. Embody me. Flare up like flame and make big shadows I can move in."[8] This is the responsibility of the church—to cast a shadow of communion so big God can move about and embrace all.

To help clarify this emerging spiraling image of communion, let's consider some of Karl Rahner's theological insights. Rahner's fundamental theological starting point is that God's grace floods the human heart and all creation. Grace is God's unrelenting, efficacious, self-gift to the world.

---

[8]Rainer Maria Rilke, "*Gott spricht zu jedem nur, eh er ihn macht*" ("God Speaks to Each of Us as He Makes Us"), in *Rilke's Book of Hours: Love Poems to God*, trans. Anita Barrows and Joanna Macy (New York: Riverhead Books, 1996), 88.

God is continuously pouring out God's very life in a free self-offer to all. "Here I am, loving you," is God's tireless utterance into creation; thus, life outside of God emerges. The activity of God, within and outside God's triune life, is pure, self-giving Love, a love that empowers us to do the same—to love God and all others in God.

To Help Make God Visible in the World

The church is, for Rahner, the visible place where this love of all—God and neighbor come together. For in truth the church reflects God's highest call to the human family to live in communion with God and all others. The church is to incarnate the "we-ness" that Christian discipleship—in fact, all human becoming—requires and discloses. Rahner puts it this way: "A love of neighbor as one's brother and sister, a communion of brothers and sisters having a love for God both as its vehicle and as its consummation, is the highest thing of all. And this highest thing of all is a possibility, an opportunity offered to every human being."[9] Where the church does not witness this, God may seem to be missing, not only in our church, but also in our world.

My brother once shared with me an old family story that connects humorously to this important calling. The McGintys, Clare and John, are old family friends who had been happily married for several years, but had no children. After eight years of praying and trying to conceive, Clare and John were blessed with beautiful twins, Michael and Margaret. To say they were greatly loved is an understatement, but that also meant they were terribly spoiled. By the time they were five and the "joy of their parents' lives," they were also beyond their control. Time-

---

[9]Karl Rahner, *The Love of Jesus and the Love of Neighbor* (New York: Crossroad, 1983), 104.

outs, cajoling, withholding treats and playtime—the list of attempts to correct them goes on. Nothing seemed to work. Both at school and in the neighborhood, if there was trouble brewing, Margaret and Michael were in the middle of it. Finally, in desperation, Clare and John spoke with Monsignor Mulligan after church one Sunday morning to ask if there was any way he could help. Monsignor agreed to meet with the nine-year-old siblings separately the following Saturday in the rectory. Saturday arrived, and little Margaret, who had the first appointment, rang the rectory doorbell at 11:00 a.m. to meet with the pastor. She was ushered into a parlor, where Monsignor Mulligan came to greet her. After a brief time, Monsignor Mulligan asked, "Margaret, where is God?" Margaret looked at the priest, fidgeted in her chair a little, but said nothing. A few minutes later, Monsignor asked again: "Margaret, I'm asking again, where is God?" This time Margaret got rather nervous, turned red in the face, but never said a word. Growing impatient, Monsignor Mulligan looked glaringly at young Margaret and asked a third time: "Margaret, I'll not ask again: Tell me, where is God?" Frightened out of her wits, Margaret jumped out of the chair, ran out of the rectory, up the hill toward home. Once in the house, she climbed the stairs, found her bedroom and sat on the floor of her closet with the door shut. Time passed, but no one saw Margaret. Michael was growing worried; it was almost time for his meeting. Having searched everywhere for his twin companion in mischief, he opened Margaret's closet door to find her sobbing on the floor. "Margaret, what happened?" Michael pleaded. "Oh, Michael, it's even worse than we thought," Margaret sighed. "God is missing, and they think we took Him."

We may safely say that God is not missing. But do we not bear some responsibility that so many have not encountered this selfless face of compassion, which is God's very nature, present in us, as church? Flowing from Rahner's remarkable influence on the documents of the Second Vatican Council, I'd like to suggest four spatial dimensions as directions to set our gaze over the next four chapters—to look for notions of the "highest thing" that church as communion inspires in and requires of us. In a way, these chapters will help shape an answer to Monsignor Mulligan's question, "Where is God?"

An Invitation to Look

I will be inviting us to look up, to look around, to look beyond and to look down as the life of our triune God beckons us. Thus, we may deepen and expand that dynamic energy of communion that undergirds and directs our lives in and as the church (see Eph 3:18–19). My great hope is that a deeper understanding of *communion* in its various dimensions can and will prevent the notion from collapsing in on itself and prevent us from thinking that *communion* and community are absolutely synonymous. The full expanse of communion is always beyond our grasp. It is the desire, placed in us by the Divine energy of God's triune life, the sacred intuition that this is how the world ought to be, that gives us both the vision and the will to help bring this communion life of unity-in-diversity to visible expression in human history. We fall short of actualizing fully God's gift of communion, but those glimpses of oneness, that we are given, undergird and direct our efforts to make this dream of God as realizable as possible. This is holy work entrusted to our church for our world. But by collapsing *communion* into our limited version of community, our particular church, even the achievement of a world community, veers in a dangerous direction. It labors under the pretense that we understand, more than we do, the Holy Mystery in which we participate. This means that when we seek to understand the church as communion, we will sustain the tension between a present reality and a future fulfillment, a work in progress, the gift and task entrusted to us as a pilgrim people on the way. There is no perfect church; there is no perfect community. Communion in God's compassion transcends the church; it has no bounds.

Likewise, our limited sense of what compassion means is dwarfed before the inexhaustible capacity that is the Divine Lover. We can only point to and hope to mirror God's life—God's full size is always an aspiration beyond our attainment, beyond our imagination. Nonetheless, God delights in our longing, since God placed that infinite longing within us.

The fourfold dimensions of communion in the life of our triune God remind us of the nature of the Church as Mystery (*mysterion*) and Sacrament (*sacramentum*) whose mission is to serve as sign and instrument—the first fruit of the "Kingdom of God" (*basileia)* in human history. As a Mystery of God's self-giving, *rechem* love, we embody the Trinitarian life of *communion* in ways that spiral forth in vertical, horizontal, eschatological (God's absolute future), and kenotic (self-emptying) dimensions. This dynamic spiraling of communion will invites us: (1) to look up—to receive communion as gift; (2) to look around—to share communion in our concrete care for one another; (3) to look beyond—to serve communion in our far-flung mission for the coming reign of God; and (4) to look down—to fall into or to surrender our lives and our communities into the ever greater Mystery that divine/human communion is.

Because God is always and everywhere taking the initiative in loving us and this world, we take our place, "stay at our posts," awake and open to what God desires to pour into our waiting hearts, personally and ecclesially. The God who loves us so lavishly continuously longs to come to us; to make of us Love's dwelling place. Such a posture invites us "to look up"; it's time now to consider the vertical dimension of communion.

Conversation Starters

1. As you reflect on your personal experience of the church, can you share a memory that comes back to you, positive or negative? How has that memory shaped you in the present?

2. What "wounds" or abuses do you see in the church, which have made it difficult for you to love or feel connected to it? How do you respond to the thought of loving the church in its sinfulness?

3. So many good, loving people have left the church in its present, institutional form. How does the spiraling dynamic of communion in God's compassion include everyone inside and outside the church's social structures?

7

The Vertical Dimension
of Communion

Look Up to Receive the Gift

Retrieving an Ancient Understanding
of the Church as Communion

As Christians, we do not believe in a static God, distant and removed from creation, but rather a relational Trinity of love, identified as compassion, poured out that all life might flow forth. Rather than an all-powerful Ruler seated on a throne, we will consider the image of a dynamic spiral to suggest God's irrevocable, loving self-offer continuously giving and sustaining life in all its forms. Try to imagine and experience this ever-active love energy stirring you, as these four dimensions of communion unfold. The question to pursue is what this dynamism of compassion does in us and to us for the sake of all life. Who are we, as church, becoming? How does compassion inform my life and shape the church?

Before exploring the vertical dimension of communion, I'd like to situate it in a larger context of the church's self-understanding emerging from Vatican II. The primary document to express the identity of the church is the Dogmatic

Constitution, *Lumen Gentium* (*LG*). Its very first chapter is titled "Church as Mystery," a mystery originating in the very triune life of God, Father, Son, and Holy Spirit. The second chapter of that same document refers to the church as "The People of God." Both concepts have tremendous significance in grasping something of the mystery of the church as a divine/human reality, sharing both visible and invisible elements.[1] But far more important to me presently is that the church deepen its understanding and commitment to become this outpoured life of compassion, received as gift from our ever-approaching triune God (vertical communion) and pouring it out in turn on those around us (horizontal communion)—those who come into our everyday lives.

Twenty years after the Second Vatican Council, Pope John Paul II called an Extraordinary Synod of Bishops in 1985 to assess its reception in the life of the church. By this time, a consensus had been reached by the vast majority of local churches that the idea of the church as a communion, reclaimed from its earliest centuries, was the best way for the church to understand its identity and mission (See *LG*, 1). What became more problematic, however, was a certain struggle, evident at and prior to the synod, that two understandings of the church as communion were operative and dominant in separate groups.

There were those bishops, like Cardinal Ratzinger (later Pope Benedict XVI), who understood the primary meaning of communion as vertical communion. The human was

---

[1] *Lumen Gentium* I:8 suggests the analogy of the incarnation as fitting to speak about both these elements constituting the church. One cannot separate either element, though they can and must be distinguished. Just as the mystery of the incarnation declares that Jesus the Christ is one hundred percent human and one hundred percent divine, so with the church. One cannot say where the divine ends and the human begins, since both elements co-inhere. How difficult it is for us to grasp this mystery and refuse to reduce the church to either one. "It's God's church," we may hear it said. "Yes, but . . . ." it's also human and we are one hundred percent invested in its becoming what God desires . . . a bearer of compassion for all without exception. It's essential to keep this mystery in mind.

invited to participate in the Mystery of God's own triune life, which came to the community of believers in worship and adoration, particularly the church's sacramental life. The experience of communion was a freely given, pure gift of God. These bishops expressed concern that this vertical dimension of communion was being overlooked in favor of a horizontal understanding of communion as an experience of human belonging, shared among the gathered people of God, an empowering and popular image emerging from the documents of Vatican II. An avid supporter of this horizontal dimension of communion was the Belgian bishop, Cardinal Godfried Danneels, who believed that implications for this dimension, and structures needed to support it, had not been taken seriously. Without the willingness to adapt new structures for the church's life, the vertical dimension of communion remained the exclusive domain of the clergy and hierarchy, who claimed their privileged role as mediators of this communion life in God, which they made available to the rest of us primarily through the church's sacraments.[2]

My particular disappointment in viewing this tension was the degree to which these two dimensions of communion were pitted against each other, as if one excluded the other, the exact opposite of what genuine communion intends. Indications were already abounding that dialogue at every level of the church's life was not acknowledged as a way to further the church's communion as a social body—as members of one another, seeking to discover together how to put on the mind and heart of Christ, its Head—an argument raised by Cardinal Danneels. Ironically, this very lack of dialogical structures impeded the Synod of Bishops in 1985 from listening to the value of what each dimension

---

[2] This vertical dimension of communion likewise led certain bishops, especially a group of German ones, with the exception of Walter Kasper and a few others, to claim that the hierarchy's role in mediating God's communion in the church flowed in a top-down, Roman-centered fashion.

of communion had to offer the other and the need for both in the ongoing reform of the church.

The Contemplative Gift of Communion to Be Shared

Nonetheless, the Synod Report of 1985 was concerned (rightfully, I believe) that this mystery (vertical) dimension of the church not be lost in a naive enthusiasm for the image of church as People of God (the horizontal dimension). *How* we encounter this contemplative gift—the felt awareness that God wants to be experienced by us personally and communally as Source of the church's life and mission—was not explored at this time. In fact, such explorations were often blocked, since the many ways in which ordinary people of God were discovering this contemplative mystery in their own lives of presence, service, and prayer were not acknowledged, but feared, suspected, and many times dismissed by those in positions of power in the church.[3] How clear it is that each dimension needs and informs the other.

In beginning to consider these two dimensions of communion, the vertical and the horizontal, it is important to note that the spiraling dynamic of communion in God's own life does not unfold in any sequential order, as if one can stop the divine flow to interpret God at work in two easy steps or four, as this study proposes. The dynamic outpouring of God's relentless love, so beyond our comprehension, goes on in all dimensions simultaneously. Yet to grasp something of this energy, we will ponder, and gaze distinctly at each direction of its flow. And so I invite you now to "look up."

---

[3] During this time, I was working to promote and help nurture Small Christian Communities in the church of the United States. For eight years, I experienced firsthand the fearfulness of priests and bishops who were worried that the gathering of Catholics in their homes—to pray with scripture, to share their ordinary lives and faith with one another, and to discern concrete ways in which they could reach out in compassionate service to people in need—was dangerous to the faith life of ordinary (meaning nonclergy) people and detrimental, even divisive, to the larger parish.

Look Up: Receive the Gift and Open to the Mystery

To speak about the vertical dimension of communion is to acknowledge always and everywhere the church's absolute dependence on God, who reveals and shares God's own communion life with the church in Christ through the Holy Spirit who has been given to us. The posture of the church in light of its nature as participant in God's own Mystery is one of openness and receptivity, attentive to God's summons, as Augustine described it, in awe of God's gracious self-gift.

Throughout our world today the urgency grows to retrieve an awareness of life as mystery. Everything is more than it appears. Have you sensed this in your own life? Take some time to reflect on and savor all that you know but cannot fully comprehend. You know intuitively that there is something in life greater than you are. You believe this, even count on it. To the extent that mystery is removed from one's experience—of another person, of oneself, of the natural world, of God's very life, certainty reigns; wonder is lost, and life is flattened. To counter this loss, poets and mystics remind us that in walking among the trees, we ought to do so slowly and bow often. Yes, "bow often," indeed; that we might find ourselves "lost all lost in wonder at the God Thou art,"[4] the poet exclaims. Herein lies for me a great hope. I sense a profound, contemplative awareness growing among ordinary people, Catholics and other Christians of many denominations, people of diverse faith traditions, and so many humanists who want to make the world a better place, and take care of our fragile, beautiful earth home.

---

[4]Gerard Manley Hopkins, the great Victorian poet and Jesuit priest, quoted these words from Thomas Aquinas, who used them originally in his hymn, "Adoro te Devote." Similar thoughts are expressed in various hymns, such as "How Great Thou Art," all striving to put into words the ineffable experience of a God who can't be contained in words.

The church throughout its long history has fostered this contemplative life, keeping it alive, often in dark times, preserving it, and sometimes reserving it solely in its monastic forms. Contemplation was, for too long, thought to be for the privileged few, not the call of everyone. The urgent need today is that this human capacity for openness to the mystery that enfolds us be made available to all. This need resounds in Etty Hillesum's decision to turn inward and make room for love and God to enter her. There are not special kinds of human beings called to be contemplatives, Brother David Steindl-Rast insists, but every human being is a special kind of contemplative.[5]

How are we, as church, called to nurture this vertical dimension of communion as Mystery? To begin with, Christian communities today must understand their ecclesial identity. Wherever you are, the church is. Your spiritual vitality is the heart-blood of the church. You are church, an ecclesial cell, integrally connected with the church at every other level. This is at the heart of a church in communion. The more communities create space for the Holy to come, who pay attention to God's stirrings, who open themselves by quiet and stillness to the mystery of God, who seek to point it out, noticing, stirring up God's life, the more alive the church is. The contemplative dimension of the church's life empowers it to see its total dependence on God, a realization so critically needed in our world today. We are not self-reliant, not self-sufficient, not in total control. We depend on God and on each other to become who we are to be.

To be in God's presence always and everywhere with open hands and an open heart, trusting that God sees us, speaks to us, loves us unconditionally, no matter what: This

---

[5]See the beautiful conversation between Brother David Steindl-Rast and Rabbi Lawrence Kushner, titled "The Monk and the Rabbi: Mysticism and Peak Experience," in *A Network for Grateful Living*, in which David Steindl-Rast explains the human as uniquely contemplative.

is to live contemplatively. To nurture such an environment as ecclesial communities is the invitation of the church's vertical dimension of communion: "Look up." God longs to pour out more of God's compassion into our open and waiting hands and hearts. Karl Rahner captures the contemplative experience quite profoundly when he writes: "Prayer is the last moment of speech before the silence (contemplation); the act of self-surrender just before the incomprehensible God disposes of us."[6] What might this look like in us as church?

Our contemporary culture is busy, crowded, noisy. We long for silence and space, even when we don't know what it is we need. I find this to be so true among the college students I teach. They are both frightened by silence and longing for it. I'm confident that they would attest to the benefit they find, as they settle in to class with a few minutes to quiet down, to declutter their hearts and minds of all they are carrying, so that they can open up to the God who wants to be present in the thinking we do together, in the questions raised, and in the conversations shared.

In coming together as church, particularly, we have every opportunity to slow down, to acknowledge in the silence, which precedes and follows words, our total dependence on the God, whose compassion and mercy wrap around us. To be in this humble, waiting stance together is such a precious gift. I am convinced that the church as a gathered body needs to do a better job of providing a contemplative space where silence and waiting on God are an integral part of communal prayer and worship. What appears to be empty space and waste of time are critically needed in our expedient society, especially by those of us who resist it most. To do this together provides a way and a witness to support a change of heart.

---

[6]Karl Rahner and Karl-Heinz Weger, *Christian at the Crossroads* (New York: Seabury Press, 1974), 53.

Strengthened by Others to Receive God's Self-Gift

Have you experienced for yourself how the faith of others strengthens you? Just recently, I was profoundly aware once again of this gift. While participating in a Taizé Prayer around the Cross, I was moved by the faith of the group. The rhythmically repeated chanting of prayers, like "Come and fill our hearts with Your peace, You, alone, O God, are holy," followed by silence and slowly cadenced reflective readings opened many to the invitation to come to the cross in quiet adoration. As small groups knelt around a very large wooden cross, deep faith and longing for God felt palpable. The communal life provided such a welcoming space for God to come and find us, as we sang together the words of St. Clare of Assisi, "Gaze upon your Lord; gaze upon his face. Gaze upon the One, who holds you in God's embrace." Yes, the contemplative gift flooded our hearts individually, but also communally. I feel confident that it flowed out into our troubled world that Friday evening, and is still being felt somewhere by someone in need. Whenever God gives us more of God, this outpouring is always intended for others. "Feed my sheep" was not intended by the Risen Christ only for Peter.

We are innately communal as human beings. To witness this truth, the church exists only as a corporate reality, many members all in need of the other. Still the question remains, how do we know if God comes in response to our communal openness and waiting? What does it look like when God disposes of us after our act of self-surrender?

First, it looks like fidelity. I suggest that faithfulness to this contemplative dimension of communion keeps the church humble. All we are asked to do is show up, open up, look up—trusting that God will come. We understand so little of the deep connections we share with all others in this one great adventure of Life. Contemplative awareness holds on to the belief that my presence before God makes a difference in others' lives; a difference that I may never realize in my earthbound form. Though I may feel nothing experientially in my prayer, I may be the reason why a sudden change of heart prevents some evil another might have done; my presence before the God of Holy Mystery may open another heart to selflessness, when it might have been tempted to close in on itself. We affect the whole of life; shift the very energy of the cosmos, more than we know. Science now concurs with what contemplation has known all along.

Though the gift of contemplative presence can often be seen by others in its fruits, this vertical dimension of communion focuses us on God alone. It keeps us, as church, aware that of ourselves we can do nothing. More and more, we acknowledge that God is at work in us, disposing of us, so to speak. All is gift. Compassionate living is but an overflow of God in us. The God who comes as the gift of contemplation helps us see as God sees and helps us act as God acts in the world. Such seeing is imperative if the world is to flourish. Chaim Potok in his beautiful story *The Gift of Asher Lev* addresses the world's great need for "the seeing of God."

> Man sees only between the blinks of his eyes. He does not know what the world is like during the blinks. He sees the world in pieces, in fragments. But the Master of the Universe, he sees the world whole, unbroken. That world is good. Our seeing is broken. . . . Can we make it like the seeing of God? Is that possible? Everything depends on that. . . . Everything.[7]

What I claim here is the responsibility of the church to become God's eyes of compassion for our world. Potok

---

[7]Chaim Potok, *The Gift of Asher Lev* (New York: Ballantine Books, 1990), 97–98.

saw this gift of seeing as the responsibility of the artist. Yes, the church, as contemplative artist, is called to see all of creation as the canvas on which God has imprinted God's very image. Its mission is to help point out, even dig out, what lies hidden under the surface of things.

Second, that contemplative gift to see more of what and how God sees enables us to sense a universal belonging to all. The intuition is more than a hint, for as long as it lasts, that I belong to everyone, and everyone to me—that I love them all and am responsible for them all. Many have described this profound experience of oneness as the fruit of contemplative prayer. Thomas Merton, whose unitive experience was discussed in the introduction, and Caryll Houselander are but two of my most cherished examples.[8] But I'd like to share two less dramatic ones of my own.

Experiences of Communion

As a Catholic, the celebration of Eucharist provides the most profound communal, contemplative experience. Through it, the gathered community enacts its own identity, its own mystery, becoming more fully itself in the very act of handing itself over. "I give myself to You, O God," we say in the Eucharistic gift exchange, and God, in Christ says: "I give Myself to you." To be disposed of by God in this contemplative moment is to become less of me and more of Christ. The living God and all whom God loves live in me.

---

[8]Thomas Merton's "Fourth and Walnut experience" is well known. Recorded in his journal, *Conjectures of a Guilty Bystander*, Merton shares an experience of communion he had seventeen years after joining the Cistercian Abbey of Geth-semani. Caryll Houselander shares an experience of communion with all, past, present, and future, which she had in an underground, crowded London subway in post–World War II England, as people hung on to strap-handles trying to make it home after a busy workday. Suddenly, she saw Christ in them all, living in them, dying in them, suffering in them, rejoicing in them. She came up onto the street and it was the same there: "in every passer-by, everywhere Christ." Caryll Hou-selander, *A Rocking Horse Catholic* (New York: Sheed and Ward, 1955), 75–76.

At times, an awareness of this Mystery overwhelms me. I look up at the long line of communicants walking up the aisle, old and young, abled-bodied and limping, black and white, and I think: "You live in me and I in you," along with all others, past, present, and future, whom I may never know. We belong to each other; this is all part of the mystery that Eucharist both reveals and conceals. What is concealed is all that we cannot yet hold. In the meantime, we catch glimpses, from time to time, of the height and depth of the communion we share.

I remember an experience I had of communion as the fruit of contemplation some years ago, which still comes back to me. One Sunday afternoon, during retreat as a novice in my religious community, the Sisters of St. Joseph, I spent a half hour in adoration before the Blessed Sacrament, as each of us was invited to do. My particular time in silent prayer held nothing extraordinary, as I remember it. But walking back from the chapel, through a long sunlit corridor just before the sun set, I was stopped in my tracks, mid-corridor, awestruck by the wonder of it all. I could hardly move as I experienced myself caught up in the incredible light flooding this space. I began to cry with a burst of emotion I could not contain, so sure was I that "God is here." When I returned to the room where all the novices were gathered, reading and journaling on this retreat day, I looked at the faces of each as I passed by. I had only left them thirty-five minutes earlier, but suddenly they looked so different. "I love them all," I remember realizing so clearly—this motley group of young women, who could not suspect what I was discovering, as again I could hardly contain the tears. Only my changed behavior toward each of them, especially the ones I hardly noticed previously, could reveal the fruit of this contemplative gift that God had freely given me. Each time I have a similar experience, I return to this Sunday afternoon and link it to a compassion connection, far greater than I can imagine.

This next experience, which I claim as part of a contemplative dimension of our church's life, happened very recently. I was standing in church during the celebration of Eucharist, when I became totally enthralled by a small baby, maybe eight- to ten-months old, who was fiercely probing with his tiny hands, the faces of both his mother and his father. As he moved from one pair of arms to the other, the baby went to work; touching, twisting, patting every inch—carried away in wonder at this intimate encounter with these loving faces. You probably won't be surprised to learn that both parents fully cooperated with, surrendered freely to this inquisitive search, helping in every way they could—to turn in just the way they were being nudged. I kept remembering lines from a hymn which has Jesus say to us, "I am for you." Yes, I was watching this very truth unfold. Reflecting on this encounter between one particular little child and his parents, I saw the gift of relationship enfleshed. This little child lives in communion, a unity in diversity, amazed by the very fact that the face before him is not his own. A tiny baby learns very early on that there is another who exists besides him—and that a very sensible, prerational awareness calls forth something from him, which he does not yet even have words for. Yet his very becoming will depend on his response. Throughout his life, this little child will, little by little, discover what this means, what this asks. As a prelude, let me intimate that his life's journey, like our own, will invite him to discover that his life is for giving—for giving himself over to these others, whose faces have called forth compassion, a selfless love in him, and from him. Each face he encounters will continue to do this, over and over again. The wider his embrace of all others without exclusion, the more he will come to resemble the God before whom we gathered for Eucharist this Sunday morning. We come to be, only because we live in communion with God and with others. Consider this for just a moment. The other is not me, and yet I will only come to be "me" and lose my "self-enclosed ego" through giving myself over to this "other than me." Here is dying for the sake of life. As a social being, the act of such self-giving requires a risk, an act of vulnerability. This very concrete, sensible experience of seeing a baby begin to evolve through the love of others provided for me a glimpse of how God loves me, loves all of us. Such is the very power of God, who has made God's outpoured, freely given love available to all, without ever forcing us to accept it. A contemplative posture opens us to this approaching God, and says in return to God, who spoke these words first: "I am for you."

Communion and Vulnerability: Dispose of Me as You Will

Look with me at these parents, who make themselves vulnerable to this little child. "Sure, mess my hair, twist my ear, do with me what you will, I am yours to dispose of." My personal, contemplative pondering of such love prompts me to wonder further. Is this not how God disposes of God's life for us? "Go ahead," I can almost hear God whisper. "Forget me, push me aside, act like you've got it all together without Me, but I'll go on loving you tenderly, holding you gently, giving Myself to you unreservedly. And I'm counting on you, nonetheless."

This spiraling vertical dimension of communion draws us together and directs us to "Look Up." There, the Holy Mystery of the God in whom we live waits to give us ever more of God's own triune life of compassion, as much as we can contain, as much as we are willing to give away. God asks only that we be willing to be disposed of in the process. There is still much dying that the church must do, both as an ecclesial body and in its members. A new and deeper contemplative awareness will be needed. The God of compassion longs to show us that we belong to everyone and no one, since in compassion's embrace all clinging ceases. As St. Paul says, "Everything belongs to us and we belong to Christ and Christ belongs to God" (1 Cor). What we see, we become. What we receive, we give away. The horizontal dimension of communion flows directly from and leads deeper into the vertical. Next, we will consider some of those connections.

Conversation Starters:

1. *Have you experienced in your own life both a desire for more quiet and a fear of it? What forms of distraction keep you from moving inside to see yourself more clearly? Have you experienced a group setting where you help each other choose silence through meditation or yoga? Has the church provided for you a contemplative/compassion connection?*
2. *Without a sense of mystery, life is flattened out. How have you encountered yourself, other people or the twists and turns of your life as holding more than you fully understand? Can you see value in the "more" to which this mystery draws you?*
3. *What has been for you a contemplative moment or a peak experience when life seemed beautiful and you caught a glimpse of belonging to it all? Where did it happen? How do you savor such experiences?*

8

The Horizontal Dimension
of Communion

Look Around from Communion to Community

We Belong to One Another

To wake up to the source of our own human identity in communion with the triune God of compassion changes the way we see everything. Nothing exists outside of this divine relationship from which all life has come. This awareness overcomes the illusion that we do not belong to one another. We saw this in Speciosa, who realized that the hated Hutus she tried so desperately to avoid were actually inside of her, the cause of her disorder. She had to face them there, if she was to know peace and freedom in the world around her once again. Just as surely as God was in her, loving her just the way she was, so were those despised Hutus and the God who loved them also. Jesus spent his time among us teaching this lesson. In John's gospel, Philip asks Jesus to "show us the Father"—show us the face of God. "Have you been with me this long, Philip, and still you don't realize that I am in the Father and the Father is in me?" (Jn 6). If only Jesus left it there, we might eventually catch on, but Jesus insisted that this is not enough—we must see him in the prisoner, the hungry, the abandoned homeless—the persons we encounter in our everyday lives. What we do for them, we do for him (Mt 25). They too live in God and God in them. The horizontal dimension of communion, the test of our compassion, reveals itself here in our concrete relationships with one another.

We can know compassion in its absence, as well as in its presence. By asking Jesus to reveal us to ourselves as we reflect directly on our relationships with others, you may find yourself, like me, crying out: "I need so much more compassion, God. Please, break my heart with what breaks Your Heart."[1]

The energy of compassion comes from a source deep within; it is the life of God in us. But in its horizontal thrust, it draws us out of ourselves and invites us to "look around." This spiraling outward dynamic of communion is what shapes community and constitutes the church as the People of God. We belong not just to God but to one another. As a church of pilgrim people, we are here to walk each other home.

Coming from God and moving toward God, our communion in divine compassion calls people together, forming them into halting but hopeful communities. Compassion energy filled the heart of Jesus of Nazareth, who called disciples to love and follow him one by one, but formed them into community, where they would be known by their love for one another. Their love was to match the way Jesus loved them. No rivalry, no competition was to be found among them; the first was to be last, and leaders were to be servants of the rest. The model for community life that Jesus offered turned conventional understandings of power upside down. A scepter and crown were replaced with a basin and towel. Compassion overpowers self-concern and washes others' feet, as Jesus showed. What strikes me

---

[1]Daughters of God, *The Compassion Song.*

powerfully about making this self-giving love for all concretely visible in community, as Jesus counts on us to do, is the reality of just how difficult this is. "Go ahead, do with me what you will . . . and I will still love you" was a gift of contemplative awareness discussed in the last chapter. But when we encounter the challenge of living this out in the everyday circumstances of our life together, suddenly it becomes another story. It takes a lot of dying to self to keep love alive, particularly in the face of rejection, insults, wrongdoing, just feeling taken for granted. Dorothy Day put it well when she quoted Dostoevsky in saying that "love in action is a harsh and dreadful thing."[2] The horizontal dimension of communion tests love in action.

Community's Test of Living Communion

It strikes me often that this selfless love for all without exception is simply too divine to get a handle on. We can't conceive of a God who loves like this. A God who pours out love indiscriminately on good and bad alike (Mt 5:45) is simply too much for us to take. And so we try all too often to reduce God to the shape and limits of loving we can understand. I remember being struck by a young woman's realization of how her image of God had been profoundly formed by her father. Chrissie came to this awareness through her encounter with other people in community, as they reflected on and shared experiences of the God they had actually come to know, not some abstract doctrines they once learned. Community creates this space of welcome and care, where God can ultimately break through. As we become more honest and vulnerable with each other, we discover that our constricted ideas of God no longer work either. Our communal heart grows gradually more open and free, inviting us to recognize the

---

[2]Dorothy Day, "Why Do Members of Christ Tear One Another," *Catholic Worker*, February 1942, 4.

God of care and compassion in the ordinary circumstances of our daily lives, past and present, good and bad. Here is a piece of Chrissie's story.

Chrissie reluctantly agreed to go with her husband, Paul, when friends invited them to join a small Christian community that met in their home every other Monday. For months Chrissie remained quiet while the group read, prayed over, and helped each other connect their lives with the scripture readings for the next Sunday and then prayed aloud for one another and for happenings in their neighborhood and world. Suddenly, one Monday evening, Chrissie began to speak. The group had been sharing experiences from their childhood that flowed from the gospel text of Jesus inviting the "little children to come to him." Chrissie began to describe her experiences of growing up in a single-parent family with her father and three sisters. Her father, a Vietnam veteran, loved his daughters, for sure, but raised them by means of a strict routine of daily duties and exacting measures of accountability. She shared her vivid memories of lining up to respond to his questions: "Who loves you?" and "Who takes care of you?" to which she and each of her sisters dutifully responded, "You, Dad."

At twenty-eight, Chrissie confessed that deep down she understands that her father did the best he could. But at the same time, she is beginning to realize that she and her sisters were so conditioned by fear and punishment, that they still find it difficult to trust themselves or others. When a group member asked Chrissie if her father believed in God, she answered quickly that she only heard God referred to in her house as "the man in charge up there." Lights suddenly went on for Chrissie, as she began to see how her image of God resembled more closely that "man in charge up there" than it did a God who hugged little, insignificant people, close to God's heart.

That evening's sharing provided a breakthrough experience for Chrissie and her community. As they reflected further on how often our images of God are shaped by key persons and relationships in our lives, they began to see their responsibility to help free others, as well as God, from the confining images that enslave them. Along with several members of the community, Chrissie now volunteers at least five hours a week at St. Anne's Home where young babies with HIV and/or alcohol syndrome need to be held and rocked.

How Others Shape the God We Come to Know

Far too often I hear college students and older adults share memories of the kind of God they heard preached from the pulpit, or learned about in classrooms, that sound similar to Chrissie's experience. I find this tragic and so in need of change. Where is the God of unrelenting love that Jesus is counting on us to resemble? To think that we humans are created to reflect this kind of lavish loving seizes my imagination with huge amounts of longing. I so want to love this way. And I am convinced that sharing life with other people who have this same desire strengthens my resolve. I often ask them to remind me of my lofty desires to let God increase in me when I apparently forget. Aspiring to the ideal of giving myself away totally to God through others is a life force I pray that God will sustain in me and in others. Community is the context where we seek to grow into the self we are called to become, the place where we have ongoing opportunities to pour out this love energy unreservedly. Take some time to identify in your own life the group of people who serve as this primary community for you. One of the greatest deprivations of our contemporary lifestyle is the lack of such a support system. Despite all that we have today, without such a loving community, we are poor, indeed. As Vatican II explains in its Pastoral Constitution, *Gaudium et Spes*, "God does not intend to save us as individuals, but as a family" (*GS*, 32).

Community as the Context
for Self-Discovery and Self-Gift

In my own life, I have discovered so much about myself in the dynamic of community life, things I am sure I could never have learned in isolation. Without a doubt, community has been for me where the rubber hits the road, where lofty aspirations are tested in the caldron of relationships, where I've encountered others and myself in all our strengths and limitations. Not only have I spent years now living in community, but I have spent most of my life in the church nurturing this horizontal dimension of the church's communion life. It is for me the clearest domain where all four dynamics of communion actually co-inhere, where the one most dramatically needs the energy of the other three. Let me try an example from my own life.

A number of years ago, during a congregational chapter,[3] we engaged in a prayer that included the invitation to look around the room. There were close to four hundred people gathered. "Is there anyone here with whom you do not feel at one, someone whose forgiveness you want to seek or to whom you would like to extend it here and now?" we were asked. After a few minutes of silence, the neat, little table groups of eight began slowly to break up, as people walked away in search of one with whom to hold this sacred meeting. I knew immediately that there was only one person who fit this descriptive invitation for me. I could feel the risk factor mounting within me. By the grace of God, we sought each other out, neither of us knowing for sure that the other felt any need for such a conversation. As we faced each other, humbly and honestly, we shared the

---

[3]A congregational chapter is a formal, ecclesial event of religious congregations. It is the primary way congregations govern themselves. Taking place every four to six years, this corporate gathering provides time to assess the past and set direction for the future.

mutual hurt we had experienced, and the truth that neither of us wanted to hold any grudge against the other. Even more, we both wanted to be able to celebrate genuinely and rejoice wholeheartedly in the good that each of us believed the other was doing in the years since we had lived in the same local community together. The vulnerability each of us demonstrated and the responsibility each took for the hurt experienced by the other was a profound gift exchange. That brief encounter opened my heart to a new experience of compassion and forgiveness for which I am daily grateful.

Only God at work in us, a felt encounter with the God of compassion, the vertical dynamic of communion, had the power to open our hearts to see ourselves in our need for God and each other; only the horizontal dimension of communion moved us resolutely toward the other; there was likewise a farther reaching (eschatological) dimension to this meeting that we'll consider in the next chapter, but suffice it to say that each encounter of forgiving love demonstrates to the world at large that there exists another way beyond grudge-holding, divisions, and retaliation, and somehow I believe this energy is effective in tilting the world toward good, even when others know nothing about it. Finally, the kenotic power of communion helped us forget about the self, let go of some of our pride and self-protection, in order to become vulnerable enough to yield our lives into the hands of the other.

Communion in God's triune life must not remain a lofty feeling or religious ideal. Concrete, historical communities must exist to be the visible, human embodiments of this divine life. The divine component of the church never lives in isolation from its human structures, since the two partners, one human and one divine, mutually co-constitute the church. This is why it is appropriate to speak of the church in theological categories as the Holy People of God, the Mystical Body of Christ, and the Dwelling Place of the Holy Spirit. But it is necessary simultaneously to recognize this same church as a social institution with all the distinguishing characteristics of human organizations, in need of changing and reforming themselves throughout history.

Forming Community as Communion Made Visible

The mission entrusted to the church requires that its institutional structures accommodate themselves to the changing needs of each historical time and place. I can't think of any social structures needed more desperately in this age of growing isolation and mounting fear of the other than that of genuine communities. One thing is for sure: The church as a human institution has various structural options in how it might choose to organize itself, but the option for community was never, and is not now, one of them. And where community life languishes, both the church and our world suffer. Always and everywhere, the church, as a people called out of darkness into the light, needs to promote genuine communities, where "life together" manifests God's saving intention for the whole world. God nudges us by God's own presence and action in us to take care of one another. How the church lives its mission to mirror God's compassion depends on the strength and viability of its community life, the concrete church being built up in love here and now.[4]

The spiraling dynamic life that is God's triune communion gift generates the need for ongoing change and reform in a church called to reflect God's outpoured energy as self-giving love in a changing world. Genuine communities,

---

[4]During the Synod of 1985, twenty years after the Second Vatican Council, some bishops noted that this horizontal dimension of the church as the People of God was not being afforded the attention it required. This attention included the urgent need to shape new structures for communication, collaboration, and mutual discernment that would include the whole people of God as bearers of the church's mission of God's saving love for all creation. The church had much to learn as well as teach, a costly lesson for many. These recommendations never made it into the Synod's Final Report.

which seek to live more authentically with one mind and heart, build up the church as a visible sign and instrument of communion in God's life, compassion poured out in and for our world.[5] Always, the church stands utterly dependent on God to do what we, as imperfect lovers, cannot. This God loves us passionately as we are and invites us to become ever more our true identity. Days of thinking of the church as "a perfect society," as the Council of Trent had centuries ago decreed, are over.[6]

Nurturing a Spirituality of Communion

But the post–Vatican II church does not need to start from scratch; it has only to return to its roots. A spirituality of communion defined the way early Christians lived out the gospel. In fact, the gospels and letters of Paul are best read as handbooks for community, rather than historical accounts of the life of Jesus. This is remarkably clear in the pastoral letters of St. Paul and the pastoral decisions of the early church. The kinds of social behavior to which Paul called the churches to whom he wrote, the list of virtues he affirmed, and the values he promoted provide a rich compendium for an ecclesial spirituality of communion today, one in which compassion is nurtured (see Eph 4). Pauline instructions pertain to ways of promoting a genuine life together where salvation has less to do with doctrinal confession and more to do with a way of life, where the core doctrine of God's Trinitarian communion unfolds in communities of compassion, living in God for the sake of the others. Salvation, thus understood, is a communion

---

[5]For an understanding of community as authentic or genuine, see Bernard Lonergan, *Method in Theology* (New York: Seabury Press, 1972), esp. chap. 4: "Meaning," 79.

[6]St. Robert Bellarmine is credited with using this descriptor for the church, which has lasted more than four centuries. In truth he used the expression a "perfect society" to contrast with the Protestant notion of an abstract, invisible church, which the Council of Trent, for good reasons, rejected.

event in which we are saved by belonging to one another.

Once again, I find in the poet Rilke an apt image for understanding this nudge to help save one another. "You, God, who live next door" is how it opens. Rilke continues:

> If, at times, through the long night, I trouble you
> with my urgent knocking—
> this is why: I hear you breathe so seldom.
> I know you're all alone in that room.
> If you should be thirsty, there's no one
> to get you a glass of water.
> I wait listening always. Just give me a sign.
> I'm right here.
>
> As it happens, the wall between us
> is very thin. Why couldn't a cry from one of us
> break it down? It would crumble easily,
> it would barely make a sound.[7]

That "cry from one of us" serves as the compassion connection, able to "crumble easily" the wall that seems to separate us, revealing the illusion of "them" and the reality of "us." We are here to save each other.

As we seek to build each other up, mutual respect and trust provide the foundation for a genuine life together. Listening to and learning from one another, engaging conflict, forgiving and being forgiven, collaborating and discerning, calling forth others' gifts, being accountable to a group, growing in mutual care and personal support of one another—all are values and skills, attitudes and behaviors that communities of compassion foster. This common goal to evolve into great lovers of God and all others in God is not easy for us wonderful but wounded human

---

[7]Rainer Maria Rilke, "Du, Nachbar Gott, wenn ich dich manchesmal," in *Rilke's Book of Hours: Love Poems to God*, trans. Anita Barrows and Joanna Macy (New York: Riverhead Books, 1996), 52.

beings. We sometimes fall short. We hurt each other and get hurt in return. "Forgiveness is another word for love practiced among people who love poorly. In truth, we all love poorly," Henri Nouwen wrote.[8] Anyone who has tried to love well recognizes the truth of this statement. In an imperfect world and an imperfect church, we form together imperfect communities.

Forgiveness and the Compassion Connection

Forgiveness is the knot in the thread that keeps reconnecting us with God and another. The compassion connection needs the knots of forgiving love over and over again. This lesson was taught to me powerfully by the Religious Sisters of the Assumption with whom I lived for three months in post-genocide Rwanda. They shared with me quite humbly this part of their story.

When the genocide began in Rwanda on the Thursday after Easter 1994, the Religious Sisters of the Assumption (close to one hundred women), made the decision together that they would not separate and return to their family tribes of Hutus and Tutsis, as most other congregations had chosen to do. They were truly sisters together, sharing a bond of love for God and one another stronger than the ethnic ties of their family of origins. But terror was unleashed. During this time of such unspeakable evil, when the church itself was complicit in betrayals and murder, the sisters did not sway from their decision to stay together. Five of their sisters were slaughtered without the perpetrators being able to determine if they were Hutu or Tutsi, since the sisters refused to provide identity cards. Throughout the hundred days of madness, sisters learned of family members killed, others missing, homes destroyed, while other sisters had family members who were deceived

---

[8]Henri Nouwen, "Forgiveness: Another Word for Love in a Wounded World," *Weavings* 7, no. 2 (March/April 1992): 15.

or threatened into participating in the killings. Still the sisters stayed together.

By the time the war was over, the pain was immense and the loss incalculable. So much had changed in each individual life. This influenced irrevocably the life and future of the community. In the early years after the genocide the country itself and its survivors were caught up in searching for, burying, mourning the victims, and imprisoning the evildoers that the new Tutsi government identified. The sisters too had lost some of their homes, their schools, their ministry sites. Not until the year 2000, the Jubilee Year of Reconciliation, did the sisters decide corporately to engage in the work of inner healing and communal healing they so needed. The sisters designed a process that included a pilgrimage of reconciliation. During the pilgrimage, sisters returned to the place where they were during the genocide six years before. As communities who endured this horrific time came back together in that Jubilee Year of Reconciliation to pray and reflect on it, life-altering experiences occurred for so many of them.

I had the privilege of listening to a good number of these sisters in 2006, as they recounted their profound undoing six years earlier. I met with multiple groups of them to gather their stories. The compassion that flowed from them in retelling these events was so palpable that I can't even imagine what it must have been like to be there for the original encounter. I heard sisters who were Hutu speak of their unbearable shame, which prevented them from being a compassionate presence for sisters who had lost their Tutsi relatives. And Tutsi members who confessed to feeling so weak and afraid themselves, they withdrew from community life at the very time when courage and love for one another were most needed. Six years later, as I watched and listened, I too felt drawn into the power of forgiving love as tears were shed, hearts were laid bare, and arms reached out in tender embrace of one another. The exchanges went on in ways so powerful that I can still feel the emotional weight of their impact.

As I looked around at the faces of my Rwandan sisters, I saw in their mutual vulnerability and care for the other the horizontal dimension of community revealed. The communion life of God took flesh in this concrete, historical community, where graced but sinful people follow in somewhat faltering ways the pattern of Jesus's self-giving life, bearing compassion for our world. Because of communities like the Religious Sisters of the Assumption I met in Rwanda, I have no doubt that the church continues to mediate God's salvific love for all. Wherever this kind of compassion for one another is present, the church is alive and God lives among us.

Learning Compassion as a Sinful but Graced Church

Community provides the school for learning this compassion lesson—the lesson our world most desperately needs for the sake of its salvation—its healing and wholeness. Each day community is born again because people start over, realizing that we are pilgrims on the way, falling and getting up again and again, discovering our own broken but beloved selves in a community of other weak but wonderful human beings. Rahner's hope was that the church in all its parts would come to recognize its need for ongoing conversion and reformation. To address this need, as early as the 1940s, he spoke of the church of sinners. He brought this insistence to his interactions during the Second Vatican Council and in all his subsequent writings.

> The Church is a sinful church. This is a truth of faith, not an elementary fact of experience. And it is a shattering truth. . . . When the Church acts, gives a lead,

makes decisions (or fails to make decisions when they ought to be made), when she proclaims her message, and when she is obliged to proclaim it in accordance with the times and historical circumstances, the activity of the church is not carried out by some abstract principle and not by the Holy Spirit alone, but rather this whole activity of the church is at the same time the activity of sinful human persons.[9]

Rahner refused again and again to listen to talk about sinful persons in the church, but no sin in the real church. There are not two churches—only the concrete church is the real church. Rahner rejected any idealized or spiritualized notion of the church. He continues to challenge each of us to confront our own egotism, mediocrity, and cowardice before daring to cast the first stone at the official church. The church and its members stand always washed in the tender mercy of God. "We are the holy and sinful church . . . and yet, where love is real, the Spirit of Jesus is at work. We can only say in fear and trembling: Let us hope that the grace of God is working its miracle somewhere in ourselves. Everything depends on this, absolutely everything."[10]

Communities striving to live the gospel will help promote a vision of this pilgrim people of God, holy yet always in need of reform, clasping sinners to their bosom, journeying together a lifelong path of penance and renewal (*LG*, 8). As pilgrim people journeying through history, we see in many places a broken world, we experience in many aspects a broken church, and we recognize in many areas our own broken communities and broken lives. Many of us sense that it is time to mourn as God's pilgrim church. We weep and repent of our own brokenness and the brokenness of

---

[9] Karl Rahner, SJ, "The Church of Sinners," in *Theological Investigations VI* (Baltimore: Helicon Press, 1969), 260–61.

[10] Karl Rahner, SJ, "Why Am I a Christian Today?" in *The Practice of Faith: A Handbook of Contemporary Spirituality* (New York: Crossroad, 1986), 15.

the church we so love—the Body of Christ wounded in its members, religious, clergy and laypeople. We call ourselves to refuse to be complicit in personal, communal, ecclesial, and national sins of denial, which is perhaps the most insidious sin of our day. In her biblical study of the book of Lamentations (*Lamentations and the Tears of the World*), Kathleen O'Connor posits denial as the original sin, afflicting human persons and dividing them within themselves, from each other and from our merciful God. How might it have been, she wonders, had Adam and Eve stood before God and each other, open and vulnerable, rather than hiding from God and denying their actions?[11] How would our lives be different if we refused the many ways we cover up, deny, and hide from our own wounded, vulnerable selves? How would all our relationships change if we stood open and honest, wounded but graced, before one another and before our compassionate God? The spiraling dynamic of God's outpoured life lifts us up to encourage one another to look around and confront the brokenness in our personal, communal, ecclesial, and societal relationships.

The triune God of outpoured love draws all life into its orbit of communion, a space so unbounded that differences are not absorbed but, rather, find room to flourish. To the extent that we, at this time in our salvation history, through the Spirit at work in us, build up the church to resemble the God we come to know in Christ Jesus, the more the dynamic life of communion seizes us with this contemplative awareness: in each community God lives in us, and we in God, as each person lives in us and we in them. Each community expresses in its own unique way the Trinitarian life of unity in diversity, breathing in and breathing out God's own unrelenting love for the world, made visible by our love for one another.

---

[11]Kathleen O'Connor, *Lamentations and the Tears of the World* (Maryknoll, NY: Orbis Books, 2002).

Conversation Starters

1. This chapter has focused on the internal life of the community, an essential, indispensable element, though not the only dimension of a community's reason for being. Can you identify a primary group in your life with whom you experience both a sense of belonging and a challenge to become your true self? Have you experienced this sense of mutual support and empowerment in your relationship with the church?

2. How have you experienced forgiving or being forgiven as a "way of loving" for all of us who love imperfectly? Can you explain how forgiving helps the compassion connection grow stronger?

3. Having read this chapter, how do you see community related to, though distinct from, communion? Why is it important not to collapse one into the other?

9

The Eschatological Dimension of Communion

Look Beyond to the Far Reaches of God's Reign

A Church Willing to Be Undone

Belonging to God and one another both creates and undoes us over and over again. My focus now shifts to the third spiraling dynamic of God's triune life shared with us, the church that is summoned to look beyond itself. The unbounded energy of God's compassionate presence and action thrusts the church into the far reaches of the reign of God toward a future, content with nothing short of fullness of "life in communion" for all. If God's very identity is outpoured love birthing all creation in its infinite variety, and if the human person, bearing God's compassion seed, only becomes herself or himself through this same act of giving oneself away in love for others, it stands to reason that the church cannot image this triune God of compassion unless it, too, as a corporate body, gives itself over for the life of the world—the salvation of the whole human race (*Lumen Gentium*, 1). God's irrepressible love propels the church not only along a vertical path, directing it upward toward the ever greater and incomprehensible Divine Mystery, but also along a horizontal path, which finds in the love of neighbor and the formation of concrete, historical communities the visible expression of the invisible communion life of God. Yet neither of these directions alone fashions a church in the image of God's triune life of compassion. The church finds its true identity always and only to the extent that it loses itself for the coming of "the reign of God." As a powerful, worldwide institution, the church must be willing to say "YES" to its very undoing.

Central to interpreting communion in the documents of Vatican II is its inseparable relationship to this metaphor of "the reign of God." Since God's very identity as womb-love (*rechem*) births all life, then nothing exists outside of God. The unbounded circle of compassion, another image for God's reign, embraces all. The Divine Mystery lures the church beyond itself into a future we cannot know. The vastness of God, and all that we are discovering about the vastness of our universe and the diversity of its life-forms, provide new reasons to stand silent and humble before all that bears a reflection of the Divine. There is so much more Truth waiting to be revealed. In Jesus's vision of and preaching about the reign of God, we, like his original hearers, are challenged to let go of all we think we know, such as who the righteous and unrighteous are, where God is to be found, and how God is to be worshipped. That vision, which impelled Jesus to a life of service to outcasts and sinners, disturbed the comfortable and self-righteous and comforted the lost and despised. That same energy flows from the Heart of the Trinity and continuously thrusts the church beyond itself into the domain of an ever bigger God.

The Need for a Church That Looks beyond Itself

In praying for the success of the Second Vatican Council one month before its opening, Pope John XXIII emphasized this connection, saying: "The phrase *regnum dei* ("reign of God") expresses fully and precisely the tasks of the Council."[1] All that the church is and does, it is and does for the sake of the coming of God's reign. Within the core gospel metaphor of "reign of God" lie the depths and scope of the Mystery that calls the church and each of its members to deeper, ongoing conversion to the limits of compassion or self-giving love (Phil 2).

When Pope John XXIII discerned the calling of a Second Vatican Council, he prayed that it might respond to three particular needs he saw as urgent in the twentieth-century church. First, he saw a great need for the church to become more ecumenical, to give itself to healing the divisions which for so long had kept the One Church of Christ broken into many isolated parts. Rivalry and competition had created the illusion that these separate churches had little or no need of each other. Second, Pope John XXIII asked that the church might become more attentive to reading and responding to the "signs of the times," a plea that the pastoral constitution, the Church in the Modern World (*Gaudium et Spes*) identified as "the joys and hopes, the griefs and anxieties of the people of our day ... that cannot fail to raise an echo in the heart of the church" (*GS*, 1). Third, Pope John longed for the church that he loved and served to become once again a church of the poor.[2] All three of these goals call for further conversion in the church of the twenty-first century.

Pope John XXIII summed it up by describing his own human and episcopal heart as one that burned with the desire and commitment to live and die in order that Jesus's prayer "that All might be One" could be more and more realized in the church for the salvation of the world. How

---

[1] "Pope's Address to World Month before Council Opened," *Council Day Book* (Washington, DC: National Catholic Welfare Conference, 1965), 18.

[2] *Council Day Book*. These three goals of the Council are recorded in the Letter of Pope John XXIII to the Whole World on September 11, 1962, 18–21.

might an expansion of communion's reach outward and downward contribute to this unifying work? As we approach six decades beyond the council, the signs of our times require a church that looks beyond itself to see and respond to a world in need—a world that has much to teach the church, while also learning from it. Where the church has become too inwardly focused—on its own self-preservation, self-promotion, and its own self-image—the heart of the church, its core identity, has failed in its mission to bear the pain of the world. In a self-serving church, there are far too many left abandoned by the side of the road, without the outpoured love of a *rechem* heart that thinks not of itself but of the ones in need. "Where is the church?" many rightly ask. The eschatological or universal dimension of communion may well need renewed emphasis if the church is not to lose itself in its desire to preserve itself. We need a church willing to die, and that willingness must begin with me, with each of us.

A Church Willing to Die for God's Reign

Before his death/martyrdom for the sake of God's reign on March 24, 1980, Archbishop Óscar Romero reminded the church of its call to risk itself for the cause of God and all that God loves. His homilies and pastoral letters reflect a heart that knew the heart of Jesus, whose courage was born from that same compassion. A few snippets from his homilies reveal the vastness of his care that the church itself be converted to care less about itself and more about the ways of God who is *rechem* love for all.

A church that doesn't provoke any crises, a gospel that doesn't unsettle, a word of God that doesn't get under anyone's skin, a word of God that doesn't touch the real sin of the society in which it is being proclaimed, what gospel is that? (April 16, 1978)

Wherever is a sincere heart that seeks God sincerely, there is true religion. This, my friends, scandalizes many because many have wanted to tie the church to material things, they call this prestige, they call it faithfulness to their traditions. But it can be a betrayal of the church's truth. (February 26, 1978)

There is one rule to judge if God is near us or far away. It is God's word to us today. Everyone concerned for the hungry, the naked, the poor, for those who have vanished in police custody, for the tortured, for prisoners, for all flesh that suffers has God close at hand. (February 5, 1978)[3]

The church is called always and everywhere to speak truth to power with courage and to serve the powerless with humility, a humility that recognizes in the face of every person a brother or sister. Here, the words of Pema Chödrön, a Buddhist nun, remind the church that genuine compassion consists not so much in serving people in need, as in recognizing ourselves in kinship with them.[4] Yes, compassion is the thread that makes all one. The church must hold on to its core identity in the triune heart of God, as it walks its journey to further the fullness of God's reign which excludes no one.

For many today, the central gospel image of the reign or "kingdom" of God has little meaning, emerging as it has from a historical context where "kingly rule" was the normative governing paradigm. Today, the subversive intent of Jesus's proclamation can all too easily be missed. New skills of a "prophetic imagination" need to be reclaimed, skills that empower communities to look at the present so-

---

[3]Óscar A. Romero, *The Violence of Love* (Maryknoll, NY: Orbis Books, reprint, 2004).

[4]Pema Chödrön, Start Where You Are: A Guide to Compassionate Living (Boulder, CO: Shambhala Classics, 2001).

cial order not as kingly rule, but as one where "dominating forces" wear other faces, and sit in places of power that are not always thrones.[5] Both within and outside the church, gospel values need to critique every social structure in light of the "compassion principles" of inclusive love, equality, the dignity of all—to put on that heart of compassion by which Jesus of Nazareth lived and died.

To the extent that the gospel image of "the reign of God" does not inform the church's self-understanding and incite its vision of the future, the energy of compassion, so needed within and beyond the church, languishes. To the extent that participation in the life of the church does not impel us to become the Body of Christ in loving self-gift to the world, our church, from the local to the universal, remains but potentially sign and instrument of communion in God and one another. A church, at any level of its life, that is closed in on itself, that controls and wields power over others, that denies or excludes others unilaterally from participation in conversation, worship, service, and decision making, is a church that cannot witness to or serve a self-giving, inclusively loving God.

From Pope John XXIII to Pope Francis: A Call to Re-Form the Church

Pope Francis has been clear and uncompromising in his message to the church throughout the world. We need a church unafraid to ask new questions, to dialogue with others, inside and outside its borders, to leave its centers of power and prestige and go to the margins with the compassionate heart of Jesus. Repeatedly, he has called for a Samaritan church. When addressing the church in the United

---

[5]Walter Brueggemann explains the capacity of a prophetic imagination as one biblically grounded and ready to criticize what is not of God and energize all that is. See chapters 3 and 4 of Walter Brueggemann, *The Prophetic Imagination* (Philadelphia: Fortress Press, 1978), 44–79.

States during his visit in September of 2015, he opened his Saturday morning homily to priests, religious, and lay leaders at the Basilica of St. Peter and Paul in Philadelphia with these remarks:

> This morning I learned something about the history of this beautiful cathedral: the story behind its high walls and windows. I would like to think though that the history of the church in this city and state is really a story not about building walls but about tearing them down.[6]

If we want to have a church that resembles the God of compassion, we must be willing to tear down walls, not build them! Most often, Pope Francis backs up his words with actions. His visit to Philadelphia was no exception. The next day, Sunday morning, found Pope Francis at the Curran-Fromhold Correctional Facility, where he told the inmates that he was there as a pastor, "but above all as a brother to share your situation and make it my own."[7]

If the church is to act as God in the world, then its compassion must become vast.[8] As the church moves beyond itself to meet the God who is living and active outside its own walls, new levels of contemplative awareness dawn. The church at every level comes to realize anew that ordinary people's human hungers are spiritual, and many of our human family's physical hungers are directly related to others' (including ourselves') not recognizing this truth. As sisters and brothers to one another, we see in the face of every stranger; every prisoner, refugee, jobless person, and homeless veteran, a human person who longs, as we do,

---

[6]For the complete text of this homily and all of Pope Francis's presentations during his US visit in September 2015, see the website of the United States Conference of Catholic Bishops, www.usccb.org.

[7]Ibid.

[8]Greg Boyle speaks in a similar way in his amazing book, *Tattoos on the Heart: The Power of Boundless Compassion* (New York: Free Press, 2010), 66.

to be respected, valued, forgiven, and found worthwhile. If these spiritual values are missing in our encounters, we can cause more pain than even the physical struggles borne by so many who suffer.

Expanding Communion in a Move to the Margins

If, as the African proverb suggests, "We do, indeed, see from where we stand," how might new experiences along these less traveled paths provide another perspective from which the Roman Catholic hierarchy, as official church leadership, might examine its relationship of communion with others? How might Catholic leaders better relate to conversation partners who ask to be listened to—women, victims of abuse, other marginalized and vulnerable groups, gay and lesbian Catholics, persons who are divorced and remarried, other Christian churches and other world religions who have truth to speak and work to do for the healing of our world?

In 2017 Cardinal Joseph Tobin, archbishop of Newark, New Jersey, did just this. Not only has he welcomed gay and lesbian Catholics to the Basilica Church of Newark, but he has challenged all church and political leaders with this question: "What if every cardinal accompanied a person who crossed our paths to a deportation hearing? Every bishop? Every mayor?"[9] When the church, in its leadership and its membership, steps out beyond its own comfort zone of the sanctuary, or stretches beyond a gathered people who think and pray just like them, the God they will surely encounter will grow bigger, and, if they are open, their hearts too will expand.

Father Greg Boyle, SJ, as the new pastor of Dolores Mission Church (located in the gang capital of south Los Angeles), testified to this experience and that of his parishioners.

---

[9] "Tobin Calls Trump immigration Policies 'Cruelty on Innocent People,'" *Crux: Taking the Catholic Pulse* (May 17, 2017), www.cruxnow.com.

Once the homeless began to sleep in the church at night, there was always the faintest evidence that they had. Come Sunday morning, . . . we'd strategically place potpourri and Air Wick around the church to combat this lingering pervasive reminder that nearly fifty (later up to one hundred) men had spent the night here. . . . Still, try as we might, the smell remained. . . . It was about this time that a man drove by the church and stopped to talk to me. He was Latino, drove a nice car, and had arrived at some comfortable life and living. He knew I was the pastor. He waxed nostalgically about having grown up in the projects, . . . this was his church; he was baptized and made his first communion here. Then he takes in the scene all around him. Gang members gathered by the bell tower, homeless men and women being fed in great numbers in the parking lot. Folks arriving for AA and NA meetings and ESL classes. It's a real Who's Who of Everybody Who Was Nobody. Gang member, drug addict, homeless and undocumented. The man sees all this and shakes his head, determined and disgusted. "You know," he says, "this used to be a church." I mount my high horse and say, "You know most people around here think it finally is a church."[10]

Greg Boyle breaks open the gospel story of the men who brought their paralyzed friend to Jesus on a stretcher, but who could not get close to him because of the crowds. So they ripped the roof off the house where Jesus was and lowered their friend through the opening. What a powerful way to image a church moving beyond itself by the power of God's communion tug. Walls get torn down; roofs get ripped off. Those on the outside are let in and those on the inside are set free. There is no them; there's just us, bound together in the limitless space called compassion.

---

[10]Boyle, *Tattoos on the Heart*, 72–73.

I'm grateful to have experienced a church without walls in my own personal experience traveling throughout our country. In the urban areas of North and West Philadelphia, I've seen the people of God who have been sent out into the streets to respond to needs of every kind of neighbors and passersby. This same kind of compassionate presence and action swept me up in downtown Syracuse, in upstate New York, in old city parishes of Chicago and Detroit. The churches in those places do not end at their buildings' once stately doors; the church is present where people are—people whose needs keep changing, as do their faces, their languages, their way of dressing, their understandings of God. But in each of them, God lives and invites them all to look beyond themselves, to find God in the faces of strangers they now recognize as part of them. We do, indeed, see from where we stand. If we are to see more—to see into the vastness of God's communion life—we need to change our social and spiritual locations. Our inner and outer landscapes need to unclutter; our church, our lives need to be undone.

The God of Compassion Who Comes as Stranger beyond Church Doors

Certainly, those who are in any way poor, vulnerable, or marginalized are privileged bearers of God's compassionate presence calling to us to see them today. They are the Christ we cannot ignore. A powerful song titled "You, the Christ" by the Irish Catholic songwriter Ian Callanan grows ever more timely as it reflects prayerfully on the church's call to be questioned anew by the Face of God encountered in those who seem to be strangers at first glance: "Do I know you, nameless face? I am fearful of your claim; yet I cannot turn away . . . you my own compassion's test, you the stranger at my door, You, the Christ, I can't ignore."[11] The

---

[11]Ian Callanan, "You, the Christ," in *The Source of Life* (GIA Publications, 2009), track 6. Lyrics by Shirley Erena Murray from "Stranger, Standing at My

gift I find in this song is how the words and melody linger long after the song ends. The message is so persistently the Word of God, longing to break through. Can we not hear it?

But there are others who wear God's face, others whose understanding of God differs in some ways from ours. They often call God by another name. Yet so many of them share our faith conviction that the God they have met and seek to imitate is a God of mercy and compassion, who longs for them to be transformed. How deprived the church is that has not opened its heart to learn from and reverence the faith of others. Yes, there is loss to be felt—a certain privileged certitude in our absolute claim to the fullness of Truth. This is, by no means, a call to wipe out all differences and claim that all religions are the same. Each of us needs to be attentive to the God who calls us, and be faithful to the faith tradition that best nourishes our lifelong response to grow into the image of the God who loves us unreservedly. Yet every encounter with a faith-filled person of another faith has the potential to leave us a better Christian, a more committed Catholic, a more fervent Jew, or a more observant Muslim. This has, without a doubt, been my experience.

The desire for a more ecumenical church that Pope John XXIII envisioned in calling the Second Vatican Council continues to be essential in our response to Jesus's prayer "that all may be one" (Jn 17) today. But the signs of our times ask more of us, I am convinced. Our God, whose triune life in communion embraces all, is so much bigger than any of us can imagine. I believe that we are being asked to honor humbly and open ourselves generously to learn from the wisdom of God reflected in others' faith traditions. The teaching and example of our Jewish sisters and brothers, our Muslim friends knocking at our doors and living in our cities, our Buddhist neighbors living here and around our world, Sikhs, Hindus, indigenous peoples everywhere are

---

Door" (Hope Publishing Company, 1997).

gifts being offered us that we may grow, and that our image of God may grow also. We want to mirror God full-size! God has work to do in us, and we have our lives and our church to turn over, to let ourselves be disposed of.

The God of Communion Stretches Us beyond Ourselves

Growing up in a traditional Irish Catholic family, in a traditional Catholic neighborhood, attending nothing but traditional Catholic schools, I spent lots of years thinking that was all there was. There was one truth, and we, the Catholic Church, had it. What an awakening to discover for myself that God is alive and active everywhere in this vast universe—far beyond the walls of the church that had birthed my life of faith but could not contain it. God wants more of me—more of our church. What will it ask of us to be a more authentic Roman Catholic Church today?

I was fortunate to spend a number of years living in Northeast Washington, DC. I had the chance to meet many women, most of whom went to AME churches or belonged to various Baptist denominations. Their lived faith and trust in God's relentless care for them, despite the hardships of life, particularly the dangers that lurked on the streets of DC for their young black sons deeply inspired me. Their hearts were so big; they cared for so many—neighbors' children, the sick members of their churches, those who were living on the streets of their city. They often expressed their need to share with others, because they felt so loved, so blessed by God themselves. I experience that same selfless love here in Philadelphia, where families who have had children murdered work to repeal the death penalty and reform our criminal justice system. As a way to heal their own pain, they instinctively reach out to those parents whose sons and daughters are in prison for murdering other parents' children. They discover that these parents, too, have suffered the loss of a child. The young person murdered and the murderer are both victims of the same bullet, I have heard parents explain. Such compassionate hearts have made room within them for both the victim and the victimizer. The compassion connection grows strong and pulls me in.

In Rwanda, the most Christian country in all of Africa, I encountered a Muslim woman, Gloriosa, who shared her story with me. As a small minority (4 percent at the time of the genocide), not many Muslims participated directly in the genocide, but a good number reached out to help their neighbors in their terrible suffering. Gloriosa spoke of hiding a number of Tutsi women and their children in her home for long periods of time. Then, she recalled, one late afternoon a young mother with three young children came to her door, begging for shelter from the approaching Hutu militia. Gloriosa's home was more than full. She could not possibly safely hide another woman and three small children. She would put everyone in danger of being caught. But, Gloriosa explained, as she prepared to close her door on this frightened woman, she realized that it was this poor mother's grieving face she would see that evening, as she turned to pray to Allah. How could she face Allah, the Compassionate One, in prayer, when she had failed to be Allah's face of compassion in action? The *rechem* Heart of Divine compassion wears many faces and responds to many names. I recognized it in Gloriosa and Allah. The same unconditional outpoured love invites us all to become who we are, beloved children of this same inexhaustible Lover.

Learning from Others Outside Our Church to Extend Communion and Become Compassion

I have learned much from teaching at a Catholic college, which welcomes young people of every religion to share our life and values, including our commitment to provide "an inclusive, catholic, community" where all are welcomed and each is of inestimable worth. We do this more or less well most days! Muslim students have told me that they feel much safer and at home in our catholic environment than if they were on a public campus. For this I am grateful, but it's what our Muslim students do for other students, particularly our Catholic ones, and for me, personally, that makes me most grateful. During the past semester, for example, in a religious studies course titled *A God beyond All Names*, Magdalen from Pakistan and Masooma from Saudi Arabia shared so honestly and passionately how Allah was for them this compassionate God we were studying about and reflecting on. Yes, the purpose of their lives, expressed through Islam, was to learn to surrender their selfish concerns so that Allah could use them—dispose of them according to God's Will. Over and over again I heard our Catholic/ Christian students express their gratitude and respect for the courage exhibited by Muslim women wearing their hijabs with great intention and creating prayer spaces where they could pause for ritual prayer. An entire class entered freely into prayer with their Muslim classmates; following their lead, they fell on their knees with heads bent to the floor, joined as one in a prayer to become ever more faces of compassion for those they meet each day. As the course ended and students gathered some summary thoughts on what they had learned, a good number shared their deep gratitude for their Muslim companions; they thanked them especially for their courage in modeling their faith, and not being afraid to stand up for what they believed. I know they called forth in other Catholic and Christian students a new awareness of faith as a relationship, rather than a set of rules, that God beyond all names is Love and Compassion for all, and that our lives are meant to express that same limitless love for others.

In the years since the Second Vatican Council, much has changed in our world and in our church. Globalization and technology have widened our horizons immensely. The request of Jesus to "go out to the whole world and bring the good news" takes on new proportions. Because we know so much more, we become responsible for so much more. Millions of people fleeing their homes because of war and famine flash across our TV screens daily. Every single day, refugees arrive at our shores and cross our borders and plead for entrance. Yes, these are our sisters and brothers, and the challenge of seeing them there by the side of the road is one we must take up, individually and corporately, if we understand that the reign of God is boundless compassion. The interminable suffering of so many of God's beloved children is compounded by global climate change. A sickly anti-Muslim and racist political culture, infecting so many countries in the West today, including our own, must be counteracted with the power of compassion, which sees as God sees, and does all it can to embrace every person in a communion of care. We cannot do it all, but we can and must do something. A church that closes its mind and heart to the pressing "signs of our times" is loathsome to a God who sees the suffering of the people and is counting on us to relieve it. The God of the future and the absolute future of God push the church forward—out beyond itself, knowing only that to be true to its own identity, the church must be willing to give its very life for the sake of others. This prayer, so often attributed to Óscar Romero, helps again to see the vastness to which Compassion beckons us.

It helps now and then to step back and take the long view. The kingdom is not only beyond our efforts. It is beyond our vision. We accomplish in our lifetime only a tiny fraction of the magnificent enterprise that is God's work. Nothing we do is complete, which is another way of saying that the Kingdom lies beyond us. . . . We cannot do everything and there is a sense of liberation in realizing that. This enables us to do something and to do it very well. It may be incomplete but it is a beginning, a step along the way, an oppor-

tunity for the Lord's grace to enter in and do the rest.
. . . We are prophets of a future not our own.[12]

Learning about God's Reign from Little Children

To give ourselves to a future not our own, doing our
part no matter how incomplete, risking our lives as church
for the sake of God's unbounded reign of compassion, and
knowing not where we are going, but only whose lead we
are following. To become such a church by looking beyond
itself, the church will do well to remember Jesus's bidding to
"become like little children." Just recently, God set one such
child in our midst. You may remember little Alex, who lives
just outside New York City. In September 2016, when the
young Syrian child, Omran, rescued from his bombed-out
home in Aleppo, appeared across our TV screens, wiping
his blood-stained face in the back seat of an ambulance,
six-year-old Alex sat down at his kitchen table and wrote
to President Obama: "Can you please get him and bring
him to my home? We'll be waiting for you guys with flags,
flowers and balloons. We will give him a family and he
will be our brother." In the Leaders' Summit for Refugees
the following week, President Obama read the letter and
responded:

The humanity that a young child can display, who
hasn't learned to be cynical or suspicious, or fearful of other people because of where they're from,
or how they look, or how they pray, and who just
understands the notion of treating somebody that is

---

[12]This prayer was composed by Bishop Ken Untener of Saginaw, MI, drafted
for a homily for Cardinal John Dearden. On the anniversary of Óscar Romero's
death, Untener included in a reflection book his thoughts on the mystery of the
Romero Prayer—the mystery that the prayer was attributed to him, but never
written by him. But it sounds like Romero's life, many continue to say. It sounds
like Untener's life also. May it sound like ours, as well.

like him with compassion, with kindness—we can all learn from Alex.[13]

Such is a vision of God's reign: a church of universal communion, compassion, and kindness overflowing—flags, flowers, and balloons—one family, brothers and sisters to all with a child to lead them.

Conversation Starters

1. *Have you ever felt overwhelmed by the thought of not being able to do it all? How is such a feeling self-defeating? Why is there wisdom in acknowledging that we cannot do it all, but we can do something? Have you had an example of this lesson in your own experience?*

2. *Have you ever encountered people of a faith other than your own who inspired you, or at least made you curious about what they believe or how they live and worship? Is there a way you might open yourself to such an experience? Are you willing?*

3. *How or when have you experienced church as a people of compassion sent to care for those who are in any way vulnerable or marginalized? How do you understand this commitment at the heart of the church's mission in the world?*

---

[13]Photos of both young boys and Alex's letter to the president were widely published, from NPR to the White House Blog. This excerpt comes from a posting of Ashley May on September 22, 2016 (digital edition) of *USA Today*.

10

The Kenotic Dimension of Communion

Look Down to Become a Poorer, Humbler Church

The Call of the Church to Become Smaller

Over the course of these chapters, the emphasis has been on God's communion life as a dynamic activity of outpouring love in which all life participates. The spiraling energy flowing from the triune life of God has directed us to look up, look around, and look beyond to discover God's compassion moving in and through this body called the church. A church that moves beyond itself in order to be faithful to the pull of God reveals something of the ongoing path of conversion and repentance the church must follow. The preceding chapter concluded with the advice of Jesus to become like little children if we are to enter the reign of God. This injunction of Jesus leads directly to the final spiraling motion of communion that I'd like to consider. Communion in God's Compassionate Life compels the church to look down—to become, in fact, a little smaller, more childlike—if it is to take its rightful place within God's

Heart of Love, where there's room for all, no exceptions. Herein the church first receives all it has to give.

One of the characteristics of a little child I'd like you to picture as we begin to imagine a church growing smaller is the act of being fed by another. A Vietnamese parable contrasting heaven and hell may help to illustrate this point. After death, as the story goes, each person sees before her or him two vast banquet halls, where a sumptuous feast is set before those seated together at the table. In the first hall, the guests pick up the chopsticks set before them, which are so huge, that no guests are able to lift the delicious food to their mouths. The chopsticks won't bend and they are way too long. Guests at the banquet languish and starve to death one by one. In the adjoining hall, the exact same scene is repeated, but in this setting, each of the guests is feasting, enjoying life to the full; they realize instinctively that their chopsticks are intended to feed each other. The parable's meaning is simple: the attitudes and behaviors we practice during this lifetime prepare us to choose the eternal feast where all are fed, where life is fully enjoyed because all God's children feed each other. What does this image mean for or ask of the church today? Take a minute to savor the image and its multiple meanings.

A favorite photo, which I use often for prayer, is one of me feeding my father in his final stages of Alzheimer's—the man who first provided food for me now depends on me for his food. It is, indeed, humbling and beautiful. I call the photo "eucharist" (thanksgiving) and for its lessons, I give thanks. Thanks that I was there to feed my dad and thanks that my father let himself be fed. There's a lovely contemporary hymn titled "The Servant Song," which asks "Will you let me be your servant? Let me be as Christ for you? Pray that I may have the grace to let you be my servant too."[1] It's the second part of this prayer I find most compelling—to be on

---

[1] David Haas, "The Servant Song," in *Living Spirit, Holy Fire: Volume I* (GIA Publications, 2010), track 2.

the receiving end of others' kindness and compassion—to allow myself to be fed, to be needy and insufficient. This strikes me, however, as a lesson that I and our church still need to learn and practice. You can discern its need in your own life and relationships.

One thing we know: we are all guests at God's banquet of life, a life that flows through us. All is on loan to us, ours to give away. The stunning prayer of Rainer Maria Rilke in his *Love Poems to God* suggests that he too prayed to use his life as gift. A life emptied of self flows freely; it takes on the character of God, no holding back—the way it is with children.

> If this is arrogant, O God, forgive me,
> But this is what I need to say:
> May what I do flow from me like a river
> No forcing and no holding back
> The way it is with children . . .
> I want to unfold. Let no place in me hold
>   itself closed.
> For where I am closed; there I am false.
> I want to stay clear in Your sight.[2]

To stay clear in the sight of God asks that we be willing to stand before God exposed, simply as we are—no hiding, no pretense, begging that God reveal more of the truth of who we are to us.

The Humility to Know My Graced but Sinful Condition

For myself personally, before I spend more time thinking through implications for a church called to "look down"—

---

[2]Rainer Maria Rilke, lines from "All That Has Never Yet Been Spoken" and "I Am Much Too Alone in this World," in *Rilke's Book of Hours: Love Poems to God*, trans. Anita Barrows and Joanna Macy (New York: Riverhead Books, 1996), 58–59.

to grow humbler, to unfold—I need to allow myself to face the God who loves me enough to want me to know my own feebleness and sin. Not only is this the beginning of humility (*humilitas*, derived from *humus*/earth), the truth of who I am; it is the seedbed of compassion. I know myself as one with the entire human race with whom I share this beloved but broken condition. Within our church and larger society, I must be the change I hope to see, as Gandhi reminded us.

The fourth-century mothers and fathers of the desert described a three-step process, a way of looking down, as a disposition for prayer—for a change of heart to see themselves as children of earth (*humus*). LOOK—WEEP—LIVE was the desert mothers' and fathers' injunction. The prayer of contemplative gazing, taking a long, loving LOOK, invites us to spend time in silence, gazing upon God who gazes on us with unfathomable light and love. If we stay there longing enough, we will be given the gift to see ourselves in the light of God's outlandish love. Something of our own smallness, "our penny-match of love" as the poet Jessica Powers calls it,[3] will at some point overwhelm us. From this graced looking, the prayer of tears may well follow. WEEP, our desert ancestors in faith advise us. This call to weep, to lament for all the ways we fall so short of living out of this lavish love of God, is the condition that makes new life possible. LIVE is the gift offered to all willing to unfold, to leave the land of falsehood and embrace the truth of our graced but sinful human condition. This realization is God's great gift and the way we become bearers of compassion in a graced but sinful world. This gift was given to Julian of Norwich, even when she tried to resist it, because God wanted her to be this face of compassion in the hurting world of fourteenth-century England. Julian shares this in chapter 78 of her *Showings* (Revelations of Divine Love):

---

[3] Jessica Powers, "This Paltry Love," in *The Selected Poetry of Jessica Powers*, ed. Regina Siegfried and Robert Morneau (Washington, DC: ICS Publications, 1999), 48.

Our Lord in his mercy reveals our sin and our feebleness to us by the sweet gracious light of his own Self. . . . And so, by this meek knowledge, through contrition and grace, we shall be broken down from everything which is not God. . . . When God revealed to me that I should sin, what for the joy that I had in contemplating Him, I did not attend promptly to that revelation, and so our courteous Lord paused there and did not wish to teach me anymore until He had given me the grace and will to attend. And by this I was taught that though we may be lifted up high into contemplation by the special gift of our Lord, still, together with this, we must necessarily have knowledge and sight of our sin and our feebleness; for without this knowledge we may not have true meekness and without this we cannot be safe. And I also saw that we cannot have this knowledge through ourselves or through any of our spiritual enemies, for they do not wish so much good to us. . . . Then, we are much indebted to God, who is willing Himself for love to show it to us in the time of mercy and of grace.[4]

Some Personal Experiences of Pope Francis

Each of us, as members of the church, is called to embody this communion life of God who is compassion at work in us. In each it will take a uniquely different form. Pope Francis willingly shares some aspects of the unique form God's compassion has taken in his personal life. At seventeen, Jorge Bergoglio (Pope Francis) recounts an experience he had after the sacrament of reconciliation on the Feast of St. Matthew, September 21, 1953. A young priest, Father Carlos Ibarra was his confessor, visiting Buenos Aires to receive treatment for leukemia. Jorge described an unforgettable

---

[4]Julian of Norwich, *Showings*, in *Classics of Western Spirituality* (Mahwah, NJ: Paulist Press, 1978), 332–33.

feeling of being welcomed by the mercy of God that day; he also never forgot Father Ibarra, who died of leukemia the following year. Years later, while studying the writings of Venerable Bede, Father Bergoglio learned that the call of St. Matthew is a clear example of God's way with all human beings. God first touches us with God's outpoured compassion and mercy, and then calls us/chooses us to follow where God leads. So significant was this awareness for Pope Francis that he chose for his papal coat of arms "miserando atque eligendo"—mercified and chosen.[5] Unless we experience personally the God who loved us first, freely and without our doing anything to merit this love (mercified), we cannot know who we are and how we are to love.

Pope Francis reflects on several personal experiences that have shown him the generosity of God who cares for him and each of us in our sinfulness and need. These encounters have directly affected Pope Francis's own response to this merciful God. In the light of God's boundless compassion, Francis sees how paltry is his love. He humbly acknowledges himself as a sinner, a brother to every other sinner in this beautiful but bruised human family. The grace we share is that God is not finished with us yet; we are on our way to becoming so much more. St. John of the Cross has told us that we become what we behold.[6] It is not surprising then that the face Pope Francis wears is recognizably one of compassion and mercy.

Another encounter with mercy, which shaped then Archbishop Bergoglio, came through Father Jose Ramon Aristi from Buenos Aires. Father Aristi became widely known for the merciful love of God that he poured on people, who flocked to him for counsel and confession. At the end

---

[5]Many of these personal accounts of Pope Francis's life are recorded in his biography by Austen Ivereigh, *The Great Reformer: Francis and the Making of a Radical Pope* (New York: Henry Holt, 2014), 222.

[6]Iain Matthew speaks of this lesson of John of the Cross in *The Impact of God: Soundings from St. John of the Cross* (London: Hodder, 1995), 112.

of each confession, he handed the penitent the crucifix on his rosary to kiss, pointing out to each that it was the overwhelming mercy of God who forgave each sinner, not himself. When Father Aristi died, Pope Francis shared his experience of arriving early that Saturday morning at the crypt of the cathedral where the beloved priest was being laid to rest. There was no one there. Jorge knelt before the coffin, then picked up and removed the crucifix from the rosary, now lying motionless in Father Jose's hands. He kissed the crucifix one more time and asked, "Please give me one-half of your mercy." To this day, Pope Francis explains that he carries that crucifix inside his vest pocket every day. He often reaches in to touch it, when he needs a flood of God's mercy to rush up in him.[7] To become a face of mercy and compassion, Pope Francis daily prays and then goes about his day trying to live out this humble prayer.

God Alone Can Make Us Truly Humble

It is clearly the need of the church as a corporate body to see itself as an instrument of compassion and mercy, a people who have nothing to give that we have not first received as gift. Knowing this truth is the heart of humility; the core virtue needed to open ourselves to God at work in us. Our personal and ecclesial need to grow in poverty and humility must take on a deeper and richer significance, if we seek to resemble more and more the Heart of Jesus. Yet the church cannot simply make itself humble. Growth in humility is the result of choices made through grace over a lifetime. Day by day, the church in its motivations and decisions must choose to walk the way of Jesus, as a response to God's self-gift or grace.

For me personally, the thought of becoming humble

---

[7] Pope Francis speaks of the impact of this holy confessor on his life in his book, *The Name of God Is Mercy* (New York: Random House, 2016), 19–20.

immediately takes me back to an experience I had a good number of years ago. I remember it like it was yesterday. I was a young sister, who, after an intense six-week House of Prayer experience, went to the Sacrament of Reconciliation with an elderly hermit monk, named Father Urban. I remember not a single word of anything I said to him or that he said to me, except his final, parting words: "When you are humble, God will use you." Filled with the zeal of this retreat, and resolved to do whatever God asked of me, I spent the next days, weeks, or was it years, wondering how I was to become humble. I was slow to learn that humility is a gift, and that God would give me the grace to receive it in and through the circumstances of my everyday life. I simply needed to pay attention to the invitation, each time it came, and respond each time it was given. God would do the humbling; my life would provide the means for God to do God's work in me. And so it happened and continues to happen. I'm grateful today for the ways God has humbled me, helping me to embrace my own creaturehood, my needs, my vulnerability, even my sinfulness. God has broken me open time and time again. I have seen in the process how loved I am, precisely here, in my brokenness and insufficiency. I know that this is the beginning of my becoming humble. It is becoming myself, as God knows me, and as I desire to know myself. And yet the invitation continues to haunt me, as something we must embrace more intentionally together.

How are we as church to hand ourselves over more and more to become signs and instruments of God's communion life poured out in love for all? To be such instruments in the hands of God is humbling to say the least. We must allow ourselves to fall, beyond return, into the abyss of Holy Mystery, trusting that God will raise us up. Just a few weeks before his death at age eighty-five, on August 31, 2012, Carlo Maria Martini, Cardinal Archbishop of Milan, gave an interview and asked that it not be published until after his death. In it, he offered some advice to help the tired, pompous church in Europe and America to let go of the bureaucratic structures that weigh them down:

> The Church is tired, in the Europe of well-being and in America. Our culture is aged, our churches are large, our religious houses empty. . . . Well-being weighs us down. We find ourselves like the rich young man who went away sad when Jesus called him to become his disciple. I know that it's not easy to leave everything behind. . . . Where among us are our heroes to inspire us? How can the embers be freed from the ashes to rekindle the flame of love? I advise the pope and the bishops to look for twelve people outside the lines and give them leadership positions, people who are closest to the poorest and surrounded by young people trying out new things. We need that comparison with people who are on fire so that the spirit can spread everywhere.[8]

The Compassion of God Will Set Our Hearts on Fire

The Spirit of God's self-giving love needs to seize our hearts again. We need to find the fire. I have spoken at great length in these chapters about the relationship between contemplation or contemplative awareness and the work of compassion. Both Karl Rahner and David Steindl-Rast speak of the need for mystics or contemplatives in the church of the future. We need people who are on fire—who have encountered the living God and not just words about God. God is waiting to seize our hearts and set them ablaze. A metaphor used by Brother Steindl-Rast is fitting here as he speaks about religion's need for contemplation and the contemplative need for religion. What does it look like or

---

[8]Ivereigh, *The Great Reformer*, 344–45. From *L'Ultima Intervista* (September 1, 2012).

feel like to have such an encounter with God? Across the world religions, people describe an experience of universal oneness—of belonging to everyone just as everyone and everything belongs to us. This spiritual experience is the foundation of every religious tradition, which may be compared to a volcano gushing forth, claims Steindl-Rast. The erupting lava flows down from the mountain and cools off. As time passes and the cooled lava reaches the bottom, it appears to be just dead rock. What do we do with this rock? We need to push through this crust and go to the fire that is within it.[9]

There is fire within this rock of the church. We need people, the small ones and those closest to them; we need the young who dream visions and are willing to work to bring them about, to stir the embers. This old church needs to become young and new again. But is this not the Easter gift? Are we not people of resurrection, people who do not believe in death without new life?

Seeking the Grace to Fall

Young people and those who are poor may be the inspiration we need to risk leaving what we have behind and letting ourselves fall into the abyss of God's limitless compassion. Perhaps that is why young people and those who are poor are our great source of hope. Karl Rahner describes hope as that act of courage willing "to do a deed regardless of risk or danger. . . . (Hope) casts itself into the bottomless chasm of Mystery, convinced that there it will find the solitary, unquaking ground of its own existence."[10] Anyone who has risked one's very self in loving another knows—falling in love requires letting oneself fall. The deci-

---

[9]David Steindl-Rast, "The Monk and the Rabbi," from *Lunch with Bokara*. For the complete program, visit www.cemproductions.org.

[10]Karl Rahner, *The Practice of Faith: A Handbook of Contemporary Spirituality* (New York, Crossroad, 1986), 248, 253.

sion to risk oneself is rooted in the hope that Someone will catch me. Ultimately, God is the falling in our loving—the dynamic energy drawing us downward toward God and one another in self-gift. And so our prayer as church: "O God, let us fall."

The grace of falling and then realizing that all you have left is the love you have to give away to others is a life lesson I witnessed over and over again among the poor people of post-genocide Rwanda. They taught me in so many tangible ways what humility, living the truth of who we are, looks like in action. Their humble posture before others and the world is grounded in their stance before God, who has raised them from death to new life. The people of Rwanda live poor and humble lives, very close to the ground, quite literally. If you want to be with them, it is essential that you learn to bend low. Images are here more powerful than words or stories, but I do have one story with its companion image of falling to share. I was not at the Remera Prison the day this took place, but one day while there, people shared with me what had earlier taken place in this same spot.

When the van picked up members of the Good Samaritans to visit prisoners as they did every Thursday and Sunday, Sister Genevieve told the others on the bus that she was having a bad day—just about making it. Ever have such a feeling? She wanted to go with the others to the prison, but she asked not to read or be expected to share her story that day. Anyone who has carried the pain of grief knows how unpredictable it is. Somedays we can cope better than others. Sister Genevieve was not living in Rwanda at the time of the genocide; she was ministering in Cameroon. Genevieve lost her mother, father, two brothers, and a sister during the war without ever learning who their killers were. When she returned to Rwanda, bereft and brokenhearted, she joined the Good Samaritans in hope of healing. On this given Thursday, the group arrived at Remera Prison, and the service began. Everyone knew the order of events, as I had come to know it myself: Singing, scripture readings, silence, often adoration of the Blessed Sacrament, testimonies from both victims and offenders who shared their personal stories as they felt moved by the prayer. The first man to speak that morning was Charles, a prisoner, who stood up, walked over and fell down at the knees of Genevieve. He began to speak: "Sister Genevieve," Charles said, "I have already asked God's forgiveness and I am ready to accept the full punishment of the law for my crimes, but I need to ask your forgiveness. I killed your mother and your father." Before another word was uttered, Sister Genevieve screamed out: "Charles," she pleaded, "how could you have done this? You played with my brothers and sister. You ate at our family table. How . . . ?" From the depths of her pain, Genevieve looked down into the tear-filled eyes of Charles, who gazed up from his knees into the grief-stricken face of Sister Genevieve, and without speaking a word, the two of them fell into each other's arms. The prison was awash in wonder! The story was recounted to me amid fresh tears, as those who witnessed this mutual falling testified to the flood of grace that filled the entire prison that November Thursday.

Several weeks later, I met Clebert, the prison guard whom I introduced to you earlier. Clebert told me his experience of that event, and how his own heart was opened that day. He came to see himself in a new light of truth. "As a Tutsi guard, I treated the Hutu prisoners with disdain. Standing at a distance, I judged them all as evil and held them in contempt. Then one Thursday morning, I witnessed Charles and Genevieve embracing each other in their pained and broken humanity and something broke in me." Clebert has since asked forgiveness from many prisoners he had mistreated, before seeing the evil in his own heart and repenting. Humility opens our hearts to know ourselves; compassion connects us with all who share our human condition; it proves even stronger than our reasoning can comprehend. We belong to one another.

Followers of the Poor and Humble Christ

Pope John XXIII emphasized that the church as Body of Christ exists always and everywhere *in Christ* its head. The church, in its call to be poor and humble, is being invited to become poor as Christ Jesus was poor—to look at the model of the humble Christ, emptied and given over, that the letter to the Philippians describes so vividly. This is the Christ Jesus, "who did not consider equality with God something to be grasped at, the One, who emptied himself, becoming as we humans are, and humbler yet, giving himself over even to death, death on a cross" (Phil 2:5–11). Is this the kind of "poor" that John XXIII had in mind for the church of the future, the one he prophetically envisioned and prayed for as he opened the ecclesial windows more than a half-century ago? Can we live the compassionate life of the Trinity without following the Way of the Christ who emptied himself for our sakes? Can we have communion without kenosis—without the giving over of ourselves, our very lives in the self-emptied love called compassion? Compassion must be the identity of the church, just as it is the character of God.

There is a powerful poem written by Christin Lore Weber, which expresses God's desired action in us, as in God's beloved Son, Jesus, and so many others who let themselves be used. May it come to describe the church becoming more truly itself.

> Some of you I will hollow out. I will make you
>   a cave.
> I will carve you so deep the stars will shine
>   in your darkness.
> You will be a bowl. You will be the cup in the rock
>   collecting rain.

I will do this because the world needs the
   hollowness of you.
I will do this for the space you will be.
I will do this because you must be large. A passage.
People will find their way through you.
A bowl—people will eat from you
and their hunger will not weaken them
   to death. . . .

Light will flow in your hollowing . . .
The round open center of you will be radiant.
I will call you brilliant one. I will call you
   transformed.[11]

A church that is hollowed out, for this we pray. The world needs this hollowness to provide space where all can find a place of belonging. What a grace to let God do this purifying work in the body of Christ, the church as social body, today! In light of the sex-abuse scandal and its cover-up in our Roman Catholic Church; in the ongoing, divisive, fear-inflicted search for terrorists (outside of ourselves) that is rampant in this post-9/11 world; and in an ever-growing national and global culture of lies and deceit, neglect, and abuse of human rights, and our earth's pillaging—I have become more keenly aware of this final dynamic motion of communion's pull downward; a divine energy that never received the attention at Vatican Council II that I imagine Pope John XXIII might have hoped it would. Now that he has been canonized, I feel sure that this simple, compassionate man, Angelo Roncalli, continues to intercede today for the church, in order that a new attentiveness to grace may lead us to become more and more a poor and humble church for the glory of God.

---

[11]Christin Lore Weber, "Mother Wisdom Speaks," in *Circle of Mysteries: The Women's Rosary Book Including the Mysteries of Light* (Saint Paul, MN: Yes International Publishers, 1995), 49–51.

Have we not been given in Pope Francis a servant leader, who himself walks this downward path of ecclesial diminishment, to help us become a church that is, like Jesus, less insistent on "clinging to its divine status" and more ready to empty itself, "accepting even death, death on a cross"? In the mystery of the Cross, the self-giving love of God for the world was irrevocably and scandalously acted out. God in Christ gave over his very life, fully, freely, unreservedly, into sinful, broken, human hands and human systems. How does the church become poor like he was? It seems to me that it will happen to the church that lets itself be carried along into places of vulnerability and risk, where it will be asked to let go of the self-protection and security that has become its pseudo-identity. It must let go images of respectability and power, the things we cling to that inflate our egos and make us look good, even spiritually good, which is the most deceptive "good" of all. A church that is humble and poor must cling to none of this. In the eyes of the world, it might well appear small and insignificant, wielding little power as the empire defines power. At the same time, a poor and humble church must recognize itself as a blessed but broken institution; one that God is waiting to heal and make whole again that it might better serve the broken communion of our world to the glory of our triune God. This we know is the irrepressible energy of communion and the will of our God, who is Spirit.

What These Times Demand of Us

Perhaps everything has been preparing us for this moment in our history. The present crisis demands new witnesses, credible models of a freely, self-emptied life in the midst of overconsumption and self-absorption, deceit and abuse of power, inequity and waste, human need and human greed. We recognize compassion as the place where all are welcome and recognized as lovingly one, though preciously unique. Our need for new models of living compassion, the witness of a community which day by day seeks to give itself over to God for others, makes me overwhelmingly grateful for the presence and action of the Monks of Weston Priory in Vermont, in whose good and faithful company I find, over and over, the fire of God's compassion in me rekindled, sparking my fervent desire to grow as God's compassion connection for others.

Daniel Maguire, a Catholic ethicist, insists that the teachings of Jesus about self-sacrifice, forgiveness, and compassion can no longer be seen as the teaching of an idealist. In fact, Maguire reasons that this teaching may well be the last, best hope for the human family and the entire family of life on this planet. In Jesus, we witness a human person freely choosing to live the pattern of a self-emptied life that other living species live instinctively. In Jesus, the human has reached the critical maturation point needed by our planet.[12] A new code for life's flourishing has been planted in us, who are planted in Christ. The life of God alive in all creation demonstrates quite persuasively the kind of divine presence that fills creation. Compassion is the cosmic life force. The very life of God is poured-out love, life freely given so that life may flourish. God has become weak, poor, vulnerable, totally given over for us. We have seen this for ourselves and can testify.

Perhaps the lesson of diminishment, so valued by the mystic-scientist Pierre Teilhard de Chardin, is most important for our powerful Catholic Church at this time in its history: "To attain to possession of You by diminishing within You," for this Teilhard prayed.[13] There are so many

---

[12]Daniel Maguire, cited in Elaine Prevallet, SL, *Making the Shift: Seeing Faith through a New Lens* (Nerinx, KY, 2007), 54. See Maguire, *The Moral Core of Judaism and Christianity: Reclaiming the Revolution* (Minneapolis: Augsburg Press, 1993), 83.

[13]Pierre Teilhard de Chardin, SJ, *Hymn of the Universe* (New York: Harper and Row, 1961), 103.

concerns preoccupying the church that center on itself. Yet the church is called to lose itself in God for others. God desires to empty us of us in order to give us back ourselves in a new and freer fashion. All our loving is but a shadow of the love God has for us. But it is in our weakness, our inadequacies, and our neediness that God loves us best. An old Sufi tale nudges the church to let God make of us what God desires. We have only to fall. Listen.

A stream was working its way across the country on its way to the open sea. The stream experienced little difficulty as it flowed around the rocks and through the mountains. But then it arrived at a desert. Just as it had made it through every other barrier, the little stream tried to cross the desert, but it found that as soon as it met the sand, its waters dried and disappeared. After many attempts at success, the stream became discouraged. It appeared that there was no way the stream could continue its journey to the sea.

Then a voice came from the wind: "If you stay the way you are, you will never cross the desert. You cannot become more than a quagmire. To go further, you will have to lose yourself." "But if I lose myself," the stream cried, "I will never know what I'm supposed to be." "Oh, on the contrary," said the voice. "If you lose yourself, you will become more than you ever dreamed you would be." So the stream surrendered to the drying sun. And the clouds into which the stream was formed were carried by the raging winds for many miles. Once the stream crossed the desert, it poured down from the skies, fresh and clean and full of the energy that comes from storms, its waters flowing freely into the waiting arms of the wide, open sea.[14]

---

[14]Sufi Parable, *Tale of the Journeying Stream*. Found in verbal tradition in many languages. See one from Idries Shah, *Tales of the Dervishes: Teaching-Stories of the Sufi Masters over the Past Thousand Years* (New York: E. P. Dutton, 1970).

As this chapter on the call of the church to serve as sign and instrument of God's outpoured, saving love for all creation concludes, I want to refocus on the image with which this section began—a church that needs our mothering even as she continues to mother us. "Every day the church must give birth to the church," Venerable Bede wrote. The energy of compassion that creates the dynamic spiraling these chapters described remains an invisible love force, but it always and everywhere reveals itself in people and acts of self-giving love for others without exception. This is the mission of the church, which lives in and through the compassion that is the triune life of God. The church becomes a vessel of God's mercy and saving love, because it has first been "mercified" and then chosen to be Christ's living Body, both human and divine—the presence and action of limitless compassion, both human and divine, in our world.

I hope you will remember that the inexhaustible Mystery of God is so far beyond our imagining and comprehension that everything I have said in these past chapters is but an attempt to express the inexpressible. But hints and glimpses of Absolute Truth are enough for God to use, as the long tradition of our church confirms. Our words and our actions continue to be the way the *rechem* heart of Jesus/the compassion of God takes flesh in the world today. The next chapter will address some of the human skills that this work of communicating "God" asks of us.

Conversation Starters

1. *This chapter is centered in paradox, beginning with the invitation to grow smaller. Find some lines or images from this chapter that hold meaning for you personally or for our church in this life journey to become who we are meant to be—our true selves? How do you understand the call to humility and its value in your own life and the life of the church?*

How does its opposite, arrogance, prevent compassion from growing in our hearts?

2. Return to the Vietnamese parable of the banquet hall. Consider ways in which our everyday life situations teach us that real feasting includes a willingness to feed each other. Use this image to offer examples of the contrast between heaven and hell.

3. Pope Francis has coined the word "mercified" to explain the realization that God loves us first exactly the way we are with all our faults and failings. This awareness makes it possible for us to love others first—exactly as they are—no exceptions. Have you experienced this compassion and mercy in your encounters with God, or with other people who may be faces of God for you?

PART IV

COMPASSION FOR THE HEALING OF OUR ACHING WORLD

Why the World Needs Us
to Recover Our Original Oneness

11

From Communion to Communication

Listening and Speaking from the Heart

What I Say Expresses Who I Am

"Out of the heart, the mouth speaks" (Mt 12:34). Most likely, you have had experiences in your life when you said something that you regretted. I know I have. My sadness in such experiences is twofold, I think. I regret that I hurt someone by speaking harshly or hastily. But I regret also that I do such things; that by not being who I want me to be and who God wants me to be, I hurt and deprive others. The counterpart to such disappointing memories is the awareness that I can and have spoken with kindness and care, selflessness, and tender compassion. By now, I suspect that it won't surprise you to hear that the more of God, the more compassion our hearts hold, the less room there is for self-concern and defensiveness to clutter our inner being.

This chapter makes a bold claim: every word we utter is a part of ourselves that we express, which to a greater or lesser degree is a reflection of the divine that we make visible to others or withhold. If we are part of God and God a part of us, then every exchange has the potential to pass on God in some form of God's infinite diversity. Early Hasidic Masters put it this way:

> Where I wander—YOU! Where I ponder—YOU! Only YOU—YOU again. Always, always YOU! When I am gladdened—YOU! When I am saddened—YOU! Only YOU—YOU again. Always, always, YOU! Sky is YOU—Earth is YOU! YOU above; YOU below! In every trend, at every end. Always, always, YOU![1]

Imagine how carefully we would listen and speak to others if we kept ever before our minds the truth of that conviction. "YOU again. Always, always YOU." We both give and receive, share or withhold, the very compassion of God in every conversation, every encounter with another. YOU, the Divine, are the subject, object, and mediator of every conversation, whether or not the name of God is ever used. Every life breath originates in and is directed by the Spirit's presence and action in us, as God's creatures. There's an old story told about an Irish beggar poet's curse that reinforces this claim. You are, I'm sure, familiar with Irish blessings, but are you aware that Irish curses are just as powerful? Here's one that had long-term effects on a whole town.

> One cold winter's night, just before Christmas, an Irish poet was trying to scrape together a little money by reciting his poetry outside a village pub, when three young hooligans, already drunk by early evening, came stumbling out the door. Hardly able to stand, they bumped into and knocked over the little cap in which the beggar poet had collected the coins from that day's

---

[1]Martin Buber, *Tales of the Hasidim: The Early Masters*; quoted in Walter Brueggemann, *The Psalms and the Life of Faith* (Minneapolis: Fortress Press, 1995), 37.

recitations. Seeing the Irish poet on his knees scrambling to find his scattered coins struck the drunkards as very funny indeed, and the laughter turned to roars. When the poet got to his feet, he stared at the three, but spoke loud enough for the entire village to hear his Christmas curse. "A curse be upon the entire county of Mayo," he shouted. "May it go on without end just like this: if anyone ever dare a gift to give, let them know for certain that in so giving, a very chunk of their soul will be lost." The poet's words resounded throughout the hills of County Mayo that night, and suddenly no one dared to wrap the Christmas gifts they had hoped to exchange the following day. That Christmas came and went, but not a gift was given. Years went by in the village, but never again did its people give a gift to one another for fear that they would lose a chunk of their very souls. The people soon lost their zestful love of life and their care for one another. Over time, very few passersby even stopped to visit the beautiful countryside. Then, word came one day that a young troubadour was to arrive the following Saturday and would be sharing his artful stories in the town center. This was cause for much excitement, since the people had little reason to get together any longer, so frightened were they that they'd be tempted to give a gift. Saturday came and folks gathered to listen to the Irish storyteller, who was full of charm and wit and wonder. The crowds were mesmerized. Evening came and few wanted to return to their homes. Finally, the young man thanked the people and announced that this would be his last story. A young woman, who had been listening with rapt attention all day, stood near the front, as the storyteller worked his wonder one more time. When he looked down at her beautiful, young face looking up at him so intently, he took off a pendant he wore around his neck and placed it around the neck of the young girl. The gasps were audible throughout the crowd, as people leapt to their feet and ran to their homes. Fear gripped the entire town of Mayo as it waited to see what the curse would bring. Trembling and with tears streaming from her eyes, the young admirer explained to her gift-giver the curse inflicted upon their town by the Irish beggar poet. The storyteller listened compassionately and then spoke gently. "Oh my dear, what the poet spoke was true, but not the whole truth. Whenever a gift is given, deep within the gift is found a chunk of the soul of the giver, but that is not the end of the story. In graciously receiving the gift, a chunk of the receiver's soul is given over too into the keeping of the giver. The soul's gift exchange can be seen in the glances shared, in the love felt, in words of gratitude expressed. And so today, I give you with this pendant, a chunk of my soul. And in exchange, I wait, aware of the risk, for something of you." With the storyteller's tender words, the beautiful, young girl reached up and hugged him lovingly. The entire town lit up that evening as they watched the couple's embrace and felt a keen understanding of the gift each of us is to the other. The young couple lives in County Mayo to this day where gifts are freely given and the very soul of Mayo grows ever bigger.[2]

The gift of self, a chunk of our soul, is entrusted to another every time we speak a word and every time we listen to receive the word of another. Who is "the me" that I reveal in the way I communicate? Communion, community, communicate—the common root is clear. The energy of our triune God who draws us into life together, where we live in and out of one another, is a communion in compassion. This is our core identity. And yet this art of listening and

---

[2]This is my own version of a story which I heard years ago. I hope I did it justice.

speaking from the heart, from that space where we are our truest selves—where God and we are one, does not often receive the attention needed or the human skills necessary to build up a world where trust holds us together in bonds of mutual care.

To Grow toward a Trust without Borders

Trust is the connecting glue in every human relationship and every genuine community. The width and height and depth of our trust are a good gauge for the circumference of our compassion, the extent of our love. A student I taught recently, a magnanimously creative and loving young woman, returned to school after spring break with a new tattoo. I said she was creative! On her arm were tattooed these words from the song "Oceans": "Spirit, lead me, where my trust is without borders; let me walk upon the waters, wherever you would call me."[3] Only a life that resembles the God who is limitless compassion can live a trust that is without borders. But the extent of our trust is a good yardstick for how large our circle of compassion is. I can't help but think of other students who have told me in all honesty that there are very few people whom they trust. They feel, unfortunately, that this is a lesson life has taught them. Don't trust and you won't get hurt. How can we change that perception and the experiences that shaped it? What must we do to expand the borders of our trust? Certainly, we need to follow the Spirit's compassionate lead.

Perhaps the greatest danger facing our world today is this erosion of trust. "Whom are we to believe?" we ask. Has trust become a naïve and unrealistic component of human relating, wiped out by the poisoning of our global and personal communication networks and social media with

---

[3]Hillsong United, Christian and Gospel Music, 2013, "Oceans (Where Feet May Fall)."

misinformation, "fake news," and deceitful, hurtful accusa-
tions? How urgently we need to combat these evil forces
with new skills and commitments to honest and humble
listening and speaking to one another from the heart! How
we speak and how we listen to one another have enormous
consequences for our personal and societal lives.

Compassion's Gift to Listen

The gift we give to another by the way we listen to them
cannot be prized too highly. In order to locate this gift in the
very life of our triune God, I invite us once again to place
ourselves in the quiet. There we gaze on God, who gazes
on us in love. In that still space, God listens to receive all
that we are and all that we try to express, with or without
words. This listening to our every breath is God's delight.
Breathing in and breathing out, God listens—no inter-
ruptions, no judgment—gazing on us with unconditional
love. Imagine coming close to that kind of loving presence
in our listening to each other, to all others. Can you reflect
on your own life and the difference it has made for you to
feel listened to—without judgment, called forth simply by
the loving presence of someone who received you in that
moment exactly as you were? "Come to Me and I will give
you Me and I'll give you back to you." Jesus's promise to
us can be our promise to one another—at least our promise to try. Nothing validates our lives more than feeling
listened to; nothing makes us want to be better people than
feeling loved for who we are. Yet so often this experience
is lacking in our daily encounters with others. The good
news is that we can get better at promoting a "compassion
connection" by the way we communicate with each other.
The urgent news is that we must. But it takes the will to
practice, practice, practice.

I became more resolute in my own desire to listen and
speak from the heart while visiting the Kigali Genocide Me-

morial Center, when I reflected on a line attributed to "the slain but beautiful children of Rwanda." I already referred to the impact of this line on me, which comes back to me now once again. It reads: "If you had known me, and if you had known yourself, you would never have killed me."[4] The stinging indictment about our past is clear, but so also is a burning question about our future. For the sake of all our world's children, will we commit to get to know the other better through listening with compassion, and thus get to know ourselves better in the process? This is the way to assure that we could then never do another harm. For each is part of us, and we of them.

In developing skills for coming to know ourselves and others better, I have found great help in the contributions of Marshall Rosenberg, Thich Nhat Hanh, Pema Chödrön, Eckhart Tolle, and several others whose work I have relied on.[5] Let me share some of those listening premises, tips, and challenges with you, remembering that the change comes not in the reading but only in the reflective practice. This is our great challenge for the sake of changing our world one compassionate conversation at a time.

To become a more compassionate listener, I realize my need for greater self-awareness and for setting time aside for prayer and quiet reflection. So much of the work we must do is inner work. In our contemporary culture of busyness, noise, and instant gratification, impulsive reactions too often threaten more intentional and thoughtful responses. We find ourselves speaking without weighing consequences;

---

[4] Kigali Genocide Memorial Center, Brochure from Children's Memorial. Center opened March 2004, Kigali, Rwanda. Brochure received February 2006.

[5] Among those others I need to mention is Sharon Browning, a former colleague at Chestnut Hill College, a lawyer by training, who has developed a website and skill presentations titled *justlistening*, gleaned from her presence and active listening to homeless people on the streets of Philadelphia. Sharon's compassionate presence is transformative. Thich Nhat Hanh and Pema Chödrön, a Buddhist monk and nun, have both contributed vastly to compassion as a way of living, *the* way to live.

we fail to listen when spoken to; and mistake countless distractions for multitasking abilities. Reflective skills, with the aim of growing in self-awareness, are essential tools for compassionate listening. Since listening creates a sanctuary in us to receive the homeless parts of another, we must do all that we can to clear out space. Here are some things to be aware of that crowd out the other's entrance. See if you find patterns in your own life similar to either or both of these as you listen to another person: (1) I think about what to say in response, whether that be a solution, why the other is wrong, or a similar situation that happened to me; (2) my mind wanders with distractions that take many forms, from what I need to do next to three thousand things happening in my own life.

The Contemplative Dimensions of Listening

Listening is a contemplative act; it asks us to behold the other attentively and receptively. Paul Tillich expressed the contemplative disposition that listening requires: "All things . . . call on us with small or loud voices. They want us to listen. They want us to understand their intense claims; their justice of being. . . . But we can give it to them only through the love that listens."[6] Compassion, as self-giving love, takes many forms; listening is a preeminent one for all who believe that "the Word became flesh." The Sufi mystic Hafiz has a lovely poem titled "With That Moon Language," in which he asks us to "admit something. Everyone you see you say to them 'Love me.' Of course, you do not say this out loud or someone would call the cops."[7] It seems to

---

[6]Paul Tillich, *Love, Power and Justice* (New York: Oxford University Press, 1954), 84.

[7]Hafiz, *The Gift: Poems by Hafiz, The Great Sufi Master*, trans. by Daniel Ladinsky (London: Penguin Compass, 1999), 322.

me that one of the ways people ask most pleadingly to be loved is by their intense desire to be listened to. What better moon language can we offer another than just being there, fully present to let the speaker's own light be unveiled. The following steps are a concrete way of loving for us, and are integral to the listening process:

1. Become focused—conscious of the present moment. Be attentive to the here and now.
2. Sweep away all self-concern, all the ego thoughts that clutter our minds and hearts.
3. Open to God's Spirit, the Compassionate One who leads us to the other and who speaks within her or him.
4. Wait with open mind and heart—with curiosity, with the emptiness of unknowing, eager and willing to learn something more about the mystery of the other.

Naming Blocks to a *Rechem* Heart

The capacity to listen to another compassionately is a clear and practical manifestation of a *rechem* heart, one that thinks first of the other and is willing to die to self that the other may come to fuller life. This desire to put the needs of the other before our own urges us to get in touch with blocks to our listening. We must first become aware of and acknowledge that we have such blocks before we can overcome them. Eckhart Tolle identifies several of these in *A New Earth*.[8] We will benefit from checking off those behaviors we recognize in ourselves, remember occasions when we have used them, consider how they have benefited us in the past, and decide if we are ready to let them go.

---

[8]Eckhart Tolle, *A New Earth: Awakening to Your Life's Purpose* (London: Plume Book, 2005), particularly chapter 4, "The Many Faces of the Ego" (adapted).

This is the kind of honest self-critique and humble resolve to change that enriches us and serves others. The following invites us to take a long, loving look at certain "compassion blocks" we need to own before we can dismantle them:

1. I am more concerned with how the other person sees me than with the other person.
2. I give my opinion when no one has asked for it and it does not benefit the situation.
3. I desire, seek, or even demand recognition for things that I do, and am disgruntled, hurt, and resentful when I don't get it.
4. I try to get attention by talking about my problems, my life story or experiences, my issues or illnesses.
5. I try to make an impression on people through my knowledge, status, physical strength, good looks, funny remarks, or possessions. Or I use the opposite angle and talk about my simple lifestyle, my commitment to justice, my care for others.
6. I talk about other people needlessly; or, I cause dissension by my angry reactions to someone or something.
7. I take things personally and am offended by others' responses or lack of them.
8. I compare myself to others and compete with them to feel important or valued.
9. I want to be seen and needed and will put others down to look good myself and be recognized.
10. I try to make myself right and others wrong through mental and verbal gymnastics or explaining.

Such practical considerations for letting go of the self and opening to receive the other serve as a grace/sin inventory to point out the Spirit's lead on this human/divine journey toward becoming the compassion our church and world need. As I acknowledge the behaviors I recognize in myself, I ask for the grace and the will to change—this is the conversion of heart God desires for all of us. With God's grace, I desire to change this self-centered behavior into care for the other to whom I listen compassionately. This is the hard work to which all of us must be willing to commit ourselves if we are to become who we really are as God's beloved children, born of and for compassion. I begin this process one step at a time, asking myself: What aspects of my "false, self-centered life" am I willing to let go of for the sake of more life?

As we have explored the compassion connection at the heart of life, so much has focused on our need to let go, to lose, to die, to grow smaller. The art of listening compassionately is no different. The key is a certain emptiness, the "nada/nothingness" that St. John of the Cross emphasized as the beginning of fullness. We become that bowl from which others can eat and be nourished. As we practice listening, we resolve to attend to these five "no's": (1) no judging; (2) no advising; (3) no interrupting; (4) no fixing or saving; and (5) no taking things personally. Those negatives will nurture a positive environment for receiving others as they are and loving them there, the only place where they can be loved. If you've tried to become this more compassionate listener, you know quite well that it requires great humility and perseverance to respond to God's grace as it guides us along this path. We must resolve day by day to practice, practice, practice. Oh, did I mention—PRACTICE?

Speaking from the Heart: Compassion in Action

This same reflective and open attitude provides a place to start speaking, honestly and humbly, as well. How do we practice a way of living characterized by compassionate speaking when there is so much uncertainty and deceit, seemingly in the very air we breathe? We pretend to know ourselves and others better than we do, since living with mystery feels unacceptable in an age seeking certitude.

Learning to speak from the heart requires the courage and humility to realize our dependence on God and on others to become more truly ourselves. We learn to unfold in every personal encounter day by day until every self-protective mask falls away; nothing can be found in us that is false. This is to grow "pure of heart"—the gift Jesus blessed with the assurance that this pure one sees God. This transformation in us changes our perception of others.

Try to remember a conversation you had that required courage and humility on your part to begin it. Can you feel the inner urge that moved you to reach out to another, because there was something you needed to say—an apology you needed to offer, an urge you felt to express your growing love, a feeling of being misunderstood or of a misunderstanding that you needed to talk through? All of these stirrings are compassion at work, moving us toward the connection that binds us as one. Any of these felt experiences prepares us to consider how to speak to others more intentionally from the heart, this place of God in us. When we let the Divine in us grow through becoming who we behold, we see the world and all creatures as God sees them. Infinite respect flows in every interaction, since we see others as we are, not as they are. To see the other, all others, as a reflection of the Divine, is a contemplative gift. Here is one more concrete way that contemplation issues in compassion, as we reflect the God who comes to meet us, to mercify and choose us again and again. This experience impels us to be for others who God is for us.

If compassion is the life of God already seeded in us, we need to experience directly some signs of this energy at work in us. Let's look at the need once again for self-awareness and reflection as key to compassionate speaking. Marshall Rosenberg describes four components of nonviolent communication, which I have adapted.[9] The four are: (1)

---

[9]Marshall B. Rosenberg, PhD, *Nonviolent Communication: A Language of*

observation; (2) feelings; (3) needs; and (4) request. Every encounter with another begins with an observation. Compassion's reminder to be open, receptive, and uncluttered by self-concern helps us observe simply what's there—no judgment, especially a moralistic one that deems something "good" or "bad." The Indian philosopher Krishnamurti noticed that the highest form of intelligence is found in one who can observe without making judgments. Be aware of observations you have made recently. Here are a few examples of observing without judging: "I never saw a *lazy* man. I saw a man who sat around all day." "I never taught a *stupid* child, but I taught a child who could not answer particular questions I asked her." To stand unknowing before the mystery that another person is frees us from making judgments about more than we observe. For example, I'm walking down the corridor of the college where I teach and pass a student of mine. "Good morning, Sarah," I say cheerfully, but Sarah never looks at me or offers any response to my greeting. She just walks by. In the act of observing, I become aware of feelings that stir in me, as an observer. In this case, I feel a little ignored or rebuffed. The feelings originate in me, not in the person or event I have observed. The person or happening I observe is a stimulus for my feelings, not the cause of them. I must own those feelings inside me rather than project a cause on the other. If I am willing to acknowledge that those feelings are mine, I can further reflect on what needs in me cause those feelings to emerge. In response to my feeling slighted when Sarah did not greet me this morning, I can get in touch with my need to be acknowledged, to feel connected or appreciated by receiving some response when I reach out to another. This need in me most likely brings up past situations in which more significant slights, or experiences of feeling ignored, happened in my life, making me sensitive to others' re-

---

Life (Encinitas, CA: Puddledancer Press, 2003), 6ff.

sponses to me. The danger of such transference hinders me from observing simply what happened here and now, and I conflate other times with this one present occurrence. Can you think of how this happens for you?

In order to refrain from judging another—in this case, Sarah—I have one more component of compassionate communication to consider. Openness and curiosity about the person I have encountered nudges me to make a request of the other that flows from my acknowledged need. In this situation, it leads me to ask: "Sarah, I passed you in the corridor this morning and I wonder if you saw me or heard me say 'Good Morning.' I know how important it is to me personally to greet people and be greeted in return by them, so I'm grateful each time this exchange happens. I wanted to ask you about this, because I would welcome your smile and greeting to begin my day." This example is a simple demonstration of making a request based on one's own recognized needs made respectfully and humbly, acknowledging that if the request is granted, it comes to me as gift, not as entitlement. It does not come because I deserve it, but because the other is a gift to me.

I've been listening to my brother John talk recently about his young granddaughter, Gracie, who already at eight years old has felt the sting of feeling overlooked, even rejected. John so loves Gracie and wants her to see that it is usually a need in the other person that causes them to act meanly to someone else. There is far too much bullying happening both in face-to-face encounters and in cyberspace not to pay attention to our cultural need to make a change. The wounds inflicted in childhood extend far into our adult years. Behind every person who demeans or ridicules another, there is a damaged child who is still hurting.

How often it has been said that we cannot hate or harm a person whose story we know. To refrain from moralistic judgments is such a compassionate work. If only our first impulse was to think "I must get to know that person," rather than rushing to judgments or making rash assumptions.

Commitments to Practicing Compassion in Action

There are several other commitments we can resolve to practice, if compassion is to be the gift we offer others when we communicate with words or by our nonverbal actions. The desire to resist selfish impulses to put myself before others (blocks to compassion) makes these resolutions possible.

1. I will resist making moralistic judgments of others. (She is so arrogant. No—what feelings are triggered in me by her behavior?)
2. I will resist making comparisons between myself and others. (He always wins. Why even try? No—I simply want to do my best and that's worth my efforts.)
3. I will resist all temptations to deny my responsibility for my feelings or my motivations. (He makes me so angry. No—no one makes me feel or do something! I am responsible for my choices.)
4. I will resist all claims to any sense of entitlement. (Who does he think he is to treat me that way? I deserve better. No—my need to feel respected urges me to make a request for respect. Receiving it is always a gift, as is everything in my life.)

When we strengthen these skills of self-awareness and take responsibility for our words by speaking from the heart, compassion links us with others. We give a part of ourselves, a part of God, a chunk of our souls, with every word we exchange. A poem of Ruth Bebermeyer, shared by Marshall Rosenberg, describes our words as walls or windows. I think the analogy is helpful. "Words are windows or they're walls. They sentence us or set us free. When

I speak and when I hear, let the love light shine through me."[10] As we come to know ourselves better through the art of communicating honestly and humbly, we discover how much alike we and others are. Compassion sheds light on our oneness. The same four steps we learn in speaking compassionately—from our heart—allow us to listen with the same appreciative awareness of those speaking to us. Empathy grows as we realize that in listening to others, we seek to receive their words without judgment also. The words they speak emerge from feelings inside them, which we may help them name, as they hear themselves without being criticized or advised. Our listening validates them, gives them internal power to know their own needs and request what they need from us, their listeners, or others to whom they will express their thoughts humbly. We do indeed become mutual gifts for one another. We are called to be compassion for our world. But to grow in this capacity, we must practice, practice, practice the art of communicating from the heart where God and we are one. The Hindu blessing of *Namaste,* which has become universalized, reminds us that "when I am in that place of the Divine in me and you are in that place of the Divine in you, there is only one of us."

For this purpose, Thich Nhat Hanh and other Buddhist practitioners recommend that we regularly engage in a Compassion Meditation that is also known as *metta* or loving-kindness.[11] It is another form of the Gazing Prayer. Take a few moments to let yourself be drawn into this contemplative practice for your good and others. Picture

---

[10]Ruth Bebermeyer, "Words Are Windows or They're Walls," in Rosenberg, *Nonviolent Communication,* xix.

[11]One form of this meditation can be found on the website: ggia.berkeley.edu. This is the Greater Good in Action Association at Berkeley, CA (Science-based Practices for a Meaningful Life). The practice of this particular meditation invites practitioners to spend twenty to thirty minutes each day in this compassion or loving-kindness meditation.

in your mind's eye, try to encounter as vividly as possible, someone for whom you feel deep love and unity. Let him or her be there with you as you express these desires.

> May you be happy.
> May you be blessed.
> May you be free and peaceful.
> May you be ever loved.
> May you be always loving.

Now repeat the exercise, this time picturing someone you hardly know. Wish them the same loving desires. You may choose someone you saw on the bus, someone in the supermarket or a church group, or perhaps someone you've read about in the news. Make the image clear and pray for them as sincerely as you can. Your goal is to open to them/ give them their humanity.

Finally, repeat the visualization, selecting a person with whom you are feeling alienated, hurt, resentful, vengeful. What happens as you try to enter this "compassion meditation" with them?

A fourth component of this compassion meditation that I think is often needed, if we are to become more compassionate listeners and speakers, is to offer this loving-kindness meditation for oneself. Self-compassion is essential to help us let go of shame that blocks God's love and peace from mercifying us. From deep inside us, God is trying to get dug out. Listen to God trying to free you at the same time to love yourself.

The Prayer of Gazing, so central to our contemplative prayer and this Buddhist loving-kindness meditation, seems particularly significant in this electronic age. We so often communicate without being able to see a person on the other end of our social media devices; yet someone is there. It takes time to engage our reflective consciousness—to see the other's face, even an unknown face on the other side of the screen. The same compassion principle empowers us to know that we belong to each other; it is a part of ourselves that we mutually exchange in every message received or sent. Recent Twitter remarks from our political leaders suggest that such reflection is often lacking and is urgently needed. Harm from the personal to global level goes viral instantly when unreflective, self-indulgent, judgmental comments are made. Claims of free speech reveal more pervasive lacks of freedom, which hurt others and breed hate and fear in a world aching for compassion and healing. We cannot do everything to change our world, but we can do something. Each commitment to practice speaking and listening from the heart is a contribution we can make to heal rather than harm another. We may not achieve a world where trust has no borders, but we can enlarge the circle of compassion in our daily efforts to share the God present in every conversation, whether or not the divine is ever named.

Conversation Starters

1. *Communication skills are significant resources for living a rewarding and caring life. Find some "tips" you gleaned in this chapter about compassionate listening that are important for you to practice. Why? Why is practice key to changing behaviors, not just hearts?*

2. *If it is true that we cannot separate where God begins and the human ends within the human person, learning to listen and speak from the heart is a "holy work." We are giving or withholding God's own compassion, placed in our hearts, each time we interact with others. Many business organizations highlight the value of listening skills in order to boost profits and keep customers happy. What deeper motivation do you understand from this chapter? How do these*

"compassion principles" move beyond appearances to the inner life of the speaker or listener?

3. *What role does reflection and self-awareness play in helping us become more compassionate speakers and listeners? Find some examples from the chapter to reinforce your thinking. How does our contemporary world of social media heighten our need for self-reflection? Give some examples from your own experience or our larger social world.*

12

"Take Care of Each Other"

Echoes from the Heart of God

Loving Large Is Our Life's Work

The identity of God—and thus the identity of the entire human family, which has its origins in that Divine source—has been the pivotal concern of this book. If God is outpoured, self-giving love for all without exception (compassion/*rechem*) then how are we to become more fully who we are, our truest selves, in and through the circumstances of our lives? Each chapter has explored this question in a particular context. The context of this final chapter is the plight of our aching world and the chapter's claim is simple: the world's healing and wholeness depend on our becoming who we already are—compassion for the life of the world. We are grateful for others before us who have shown us the way. As people of Christian faith, we seek to follow in the footsteps of Jesus, who is the Way. We believe that, rooted in Christ, we have everything we need to help save this hurting and hostile world. This is the mission of the church. We have only to live our truth boldly and wholeheartedly by resisting all smaller versions of ourselves.

But those lesser versions of the self are omnipresent and

often seduce us into thinking that the circle of our loving is justifiably small. Our work is to love the world—no exceptions. From these hummingbirds to those sunflowers, from those little sandpipers to that amazing sandcastle, the list goes on. I am here to love—this person who seemed to cut me off in traffic, that colleague who never looks up from her notepad when I try to respond to her questions, those politicians who fill the airwaves with their condemnatory remarks about the opposing party, even those countries with weapons of war pointed at us, while we in the United States do the same to them. The distinguishing characteristic that the *rechem* heart of Jesus modeled is enemy-love. To love as God loves—to birth our world anew—there can be no limits to our loving. Hate cannot overcome hate; only love can do that. Martin Luther King Jr. preached and lived this truth of his heart. Thinking that violence can pave the way to peace in our world has deceived us for far too long. Seeing the other, all others, as one with us and needed by us, rather than separate from us and expendable to us is a transformative gift that compassion longs to give us. The world desperately needs this gift from us.

Seeing as God Sees: Eyes of Compassion

How does God see our world and the human family created in God's own image? Could we ever hope to learn to see as God sees? The longer I live, the clearer I see that my vision is as wide as the horizons of my loving—but God's vision and horizons of loving are infinite.

A reflection written by Russell Schweickart, after he returned from the Apollo 9 Earth Orbital flight in 1969, describes an experience that points to the larger view God sees and longs to share with us, God's beloved children. Schweickart sensed a responsibility to pass on what he saw so clearly out there in space. The awesome awakening that he experienced happened to all of us, he insists: the entire human family gained this larger perspective of who we are. He had not been separated out by God to have this experience for himself alone. No, he was a "sensing element of humankind" out there. What happened for one of us happened to all of us. We underwent a consciousness shift, a contemplative moment; we were given a glimpse of earth from outside it. Schweickart had a responsibility now to make clear: "All those people down there are like you—they are you." We are one. Again and again, we are reminded.

> When you go around the earth in an hour and a half, you begin to recognize that your identity is with that whole thing. And that makes a change. You look down there and you can't imagine how many borders and boundaries you cross again and again and again and you don't even see them. There you are—hundreds of people in the Middle East killing each other over some imaginary line that you're not even aware of, that you can't see. And from where you see it, the thing is a whole and it's so beautiful. You wish you could take one in each hand, one from each side of the various conflicts, and say: "Look. Look at it from this perspective. Look at that—what's important?"[1]

Almost half a century later, the question of what is important haunts us still. The responsibility to act looms large, as our world aches with countless killings and incalculable suffering perpetrated and justified by the ever-growing numbers of imaginary boundaries created to divide and separate us, prevent us from seeing ourselves as one beloved human family on this one beautiful planet.

---

[1] Russell Schweickart, "No Frames; No Boundaries: Connecting with the Whole Planet—From Space," in *Rediscovering the North American Vision* 1C#3 (Context Institute: Summer 1983), 16.

Compassion Connects Us with God and All Others

If we were able to examine every ache that burdens and breaks open our world's heart today, we would find that each of those separate piercings is somehow caused by the giant wound of our human forgetfulness; our failure to remember who we are and to whom we belong. A poem by William Stafford titled "The Way It Is" challenges us to hold on to what is essential and unchanging in our fast-paced, ever-changing world. The rest we can let go.

> There's a thread you follow. It goes among
> things that change. But it doesn't change.
> People wonder about what you are pursuing.
> You have to explain about the thread.
> But it is hard for others to see.
> While you hold it you can't get lost.
> Tragedies happen; people get hurt
> or die; and you suffer and get old.
> Nothing you do can stop time's unfolding.
> You don't ever let go of the thread.[2]

It's this thread, this compassion connection, the very heart-beat of God moving in us and all around us that ultimately pursues us even when we seemingly lose touch with it. Our call is to hang on tightly to this unbroken thread that holds us together amid all the brokenness around us. But paying attention to this thread that unites us is not easy in our fractured lives and wounded world. Because our hearts are cluttered and disordered, we settle for smaller, disconnected versions of ourselves. We forget about the thread that binds us. But today's great needs will not be faced and overcome

---

[2]William Stafford, "The Way It Is," in *The Way It Is: New and Selected Poems by William Stafford* (St. Paul, MN: Gray Wolf Press, 1998), 42.

by our living in the small world of petty self-absorption, unmindful of the needs of others.

We earlier identified this thread of unity in the context of Etty Hillesum's life, as a young Jewish girl living during the Holocaust, and in that of the people of Rwanda living through the 1994 genocide. But what about us today? Can we identify something of our global context, which invites us, pleads with us, to live into a larger version of ourselves for the sake of our world today? In an effort to single out one challenge, sounding a wake-up call to our entire human family here and now, I set before us the experience of our current global migration crisis. Can we perceive that the whole map of humankind is being rewritten in the flesh and blood of our sisters and brothers; the ones who have left all that they know behind them to cross borders into an unknown future we play some part in shaping? If it is true that their future lies in our hands, is it likewise true that our future lies in theirs?

The Global Migration Crisis as Compassion's Test Today

Throughout these chapters, we have seen over and over again how much dying and loss is asked of us on this human journey to become the compassion of God that is our very identity. What then are we to learn from the many dyings and losses that millions upon millions are undergoing today? How do we see ourselves in them? What mutual gifts are we invited to exchange to live more fully into the divine/human communion we share? What will become of us and of our world? Will God's dream of a world at one fashion the path we walk?

There is so much more to learn about the complex reasons that force so many innocent people to flee their homelands today. The United Nations and other agencies have classified the mass of migrants as: (1) Economic migrants who suffer from poverty and leave their homelands to make a better life for themselves and their families. (2) Forced migrants who are today's refugees, fleeing because of some "well-founded fear of persecution for reasons of race, religion, nationality, membership in a particular social group or political opinion." Over sixty-five million refugees are homeless and seeking safety and shelter today. (3) Internally displaced persons who have not left their homeland, but are living in makeshift camps away from their homes because war or famine has caused them to leave all they had behind. And finally, (4) Victims of human trafficking, numbering up to twenty-seven million people, who have been sold into work or sex trade for lucrative profits gained by their abductors.[3]

Compassion Asks More of Us Than Feeling Sad

Nothing can protect us from seeing the faces or hearing the cries of these, our most needy and vulnerable sisters and brothers, so many of them children. But what will it take for us to express more than sadness in seeing their suffering? What will it take for us to open our hearts to receive them, to act on their behalf?[4] Will we wake up to become who we

---

[3]The United States Catholic Conference of Bishops website gives these and many other helpful statistics of the nature and scope of the migration crisis today. We remember that each is a person bound to us by ties of compassion. These people, each and every one, are so much more than numbers.

[4]A quite amazing story of someone who did open her heart and transform her life to make room for the refugees among us is Mary Jo Leddy, who for thirty years now has directed Romero House in Toronto, Canada, living with and welcoming refugees to find their rightful home in our one human family. To learn many personal stories of these refugees and their impact on Leddy's life, see her book *The Other Face of God: When the Stranger Calls Us Home* (Maryknoll, NY: Orbis Books, 2011). Using Mary Jo Leddy's book in class is one of the ways I have to make the refugees real persons for the students I teach. Dr. Leddy came to our Institute for Forgiveness and Reconciliation to share her stories as well. Yet the most profound experience I have, as a college professor, is the gift of listening compassionately to students themselves who fear their parents' deportation. Some have fathers already on lists and in detention centers, waiting to be deported. The pain of loss and separation is so deep.

say we are? A powerful YouTube video with penetrating images and an accompanying song titled "Who We Are" by Gungor challenges us to this larger version of ourselves.

> All the world watches as the people run
> from the fiercest storm to the fierce unknown.
> Will we watch and wait, turn and close our door,
> or will we be who we've always said we are?
>
> All the world watched his little body there,
> innocent and still at the water's edge
> and it stole our breath away.
> LOVE that holds him now asks for more than
>   words:
> Will we be who we've always said we are?[5]

Compassion as the Work of Mothering

Yes, the Compassionate Heart of Love who holds the young Syrian child asks for more than words from us. How will we live into our truest selves? The magnitude of this global crisis makes one thing perfectly clear. No one alone can make right this human tragedy. God does not intend to save us individually. We are here to help save each other. "Take care of each other," echoes from the aching heart of our Mother God, from whose womb we have all been birthed.

The very thought of taking care of each other brings me back to cherished memories I have of my own mother. You may pause to remember similar experiences in your own life, whether from your mother or a mother-figure. Nothing I can remember seemed to matter more to my mom than seeing us being good to each other or taking care of each

---

[5]Gungor, "Who We Are," https://www.youtube.com/watch?v=uV5JJTrB058 &feature=youtu.be.

other. Alternately, nothing caused her more grief than the thought of our quarreling or not taking good care of each other. I have so many examples, but one comes back to me in photo form. There was a nearly eighteen-month period when I did not get to see my sister, Mary Ann, who had entered another religious congregation the year after I entered the Sisters of St. Joseph. During that formation period, we could not visit each other. When I was able to attend the reception ceremony for my sister, someone took a picture of my sister and me together again in a loving embrace. What I treasure so much about that photo is the face of my mother in the background. She looks absolutely ready to jump out of her skin in delight, as she watches Mary Ann and me hug each other after our long time apart. I often reflect on my mother's face as the face of God; nothing delights God more than seeing God's children taking care of each other. We five siblings often remind each other of how happy mom must be to see how we continue to take care of each other today. As we stand around the hospital bed of my oldest brother Frank, who suffered a very debilitating stroke some months ago, we take note of mom's greatest desire for us becoming the way we live today. Of course, here we are taking care of each other, just as our mom and our Mother God would have us do. We don't always do it perfectly, but we try!

Compassion Connects the Entire Human Family

As we turn to our global crisis, we see that responses of care come in every shape and size—from government agencies at the federal, state, and local levels; international political and human rights organizations; churches and faith groups of every persuasion; human rights advocates and social services; to the host of them all working together. These shared commitments reveal the connections that bind us as one human family. Any one of the varied networking groups provides an entry point for each of us to do something rather than nothing. From writing letters to Congress on immigration reform to working directly with refugee resettlement agencies, we can put one foot in front of the other rather than become overwhelmed because we cannot do everything to remedy this heartbreaking situation.

There are so many reasons why we must learn more about the economic and political turmoil that makes life so unbearable for so many and the varied ways so many see the complexities surrounding the migration experience of our sisters and brothers throughout our world. In the process, we in the United States must face our own complicity as the wealthiest and most powerful nation in this world for the economic disparity and powerlessness that confront so many people struggling to survive in poor countries, often with corrupt governments. How can it be that some of us have so much more than we need, when others are destitute? Consider this fact alone: any of us making $55.00 a day is living in the top 5 percent of the world's wealthiest people. What effect does such inequity have on how most of our sisters and brothers must live?

Constructing the Other: Labels That Divide Us

The question goes still deeper to ask if we truly do perceive the other 95 percent as our sisters and brothers? How do we see "the other" in our midst or at a distance? In Robert Schreiter's work on the ministry of reconciliation entrusted to us, as church, he identifies ways in which we construct "the other" by creating labels that divide us from them and then justify the separation.[6] There is no "us," these

---

[6]Robert J. Schreiter, *Reconciliation: Mission and Ministry in a Changing Social Order* (Maryknoll, NY: Orbis Books, 1992), 52–53. In this section, Schreiter identifies seven specific categories as ways in which we construct "the other," and thus distance ourselves from them. I have used four of those seven categories and applied them to how we regard one another in light of our migration crisis today.

labels claim; there's only "them." A few of these categories are relevant to how we construct "the other" vis-à-vis the migration challenge facing us all today.

1. *Demonize:* We create reasons to vilify those trying to enter our country to find safety or a better life, calling them terrorists, drug dealers, job snatchers, illegals, lazy parasites who will live off our government and hard-earned wealth.

2. *Romanticize:* Those who reach out and put themselves at risk for the sake of these suffering people are separated out as the saints among us. We put them up on pedestals, glorify them, and see their response as superhuman. They are not like the rest of us. Maybe they received the compassion gene that passed others of us by. We revere them but do not want to become them.

3. *Homogenize:* Often we hear the statistics, the staggering numbers and massive crowds of fleeing people, and we lump them all together, because trying to learn each one's unique story would likely break our hearts—we would realize they were so much like us.

4. *Vaporize:* We are overwhelmed by gruesome scenes of human suffering that fill our airwaves and our social media. We resolve, then, not to read or look at such accounts. Seeing all this just makes us too sad. We don't want to expose ourselves or our children to such heartache. We simply try to make it go away.[7]

The work of standing before this world here and now, open, vulnerable, and unafraid—in this time and place where God has chosen to come to dwell among us—asks much of us. All the contemplative attitudes we have tried to pay attention to and practice are now called forth and put

---

[7]Ibid., 53.

to the test. How we see and respond to today's migration crisis is foundationally a theological question before it is a political, social, or economic one, though we cannot ignore any of these subsequent and interconnected questions. How we understand God, ourselves, the other—the very questions with which this text began—resurface as urgent and incomparably significant for the future of our world and its citizens. Are we fundamentally more than citizens of various nations, pledged to uphold those rights and duties before all others? Or do we belong to one another, all others without exception, in a circle of compassion that encompasses our whole world and excludes no one? Do we see the migrants trying to reach our shores as aliens, cheap laborers, or our sisters and brothers in need? Our answers, lived out in deeds and not simply words, will define us and our future at this time in our salvation history.

There is a beautiful hymn titled "This Is My Song," which echoes some of these sentiments as well. Even to use a word like sentiment suggests that the heart must be involved in making decisions of this magnitude. The intellect alone cannot hold all the truth we need to uncover.

> This is my song, O God of all the nations, a song
>   of peace for lands afar and mine.
> This is my home, the country where my heart is;
>   here are my hopes,
> my dreams, my holy shrine; but other hearts in
>   other lands are beating
> with hopes and dreams as true and high as mine.
>
> My country's skies are bluer than the ocean,
>   and sunlight beams on clover-leaf and pine.
> But other lands have sunlight too and clover,
>   and skies are everywhere as blue as mine.
> Oh, hear my song, O God of all the nations,
>   a song of peace for their land and for mine.

Teach us to sing, O God of all creation, a song
   of hope for oceans, sky and pine,
Teach us to love the way that ends division,
   till every land and nation love entwine.
Then will all people see your glorious vision,
   a world at peace, beloved and divine.[8]

Our primary global need and goal must be to find ways
for people to live in peace and security in their own beloved
countries. But that is far from our present reality. With all
the loss entailed in fleeing one's homeland, it is important
to realize that those who migrate do it out of necessity
and not for selfish ends. Over and over, we hear, if we
are willing to listen, about hopes for a better life for their
children, about the land and people that they loved and
left behind, and about the values that gave them courage
to risk it all. In each story, we hear something of our own
story being told. Each of these struggling persons has hopes
and dreams as true and high as ours. That now iconic image of the three-year-old child lying lifeless and facedown
at the ocean's edge, as Syrian families tried to reach shore,
touched many of us with a piercing collective cry. "This
could have been our child," we felt. "No, this is our child,"
compassion reminds us.

Recovering Our Original Oneness: The Example of Pope Francis

After reading that five thousand people had died on a
rickety, storm-tossed fishing boat trying to reach the small
island of Lampedusa, Pope Francis boarded an Alitalia
airplane to go there himself in July 2013, a short time after
being elected pope. He explained the shift in him—from a

---

[8]Marty Haugen and Marc Anderson, "This Is My Song," *In the Days to Come: Songs of Peace* (Chicago, IL: GIA Publications, 2006), track 3.

man who did not like to travel, to one who knew he needed to be there. The need to be with people who suffer, regardless of the cost, is a compassion tug that we need to experience for ourselves. Nothing changes us as dramatically as a personal encounter with another vulnerable human being. And so Francis needed to be there to embrace the suffering thousands washed up on Italy's shores. That same pull has impelled his many pilgrim journeys since Lampedusa. There are far too many places and faces to mention, but the lesson is always the same. They are a part of me; their suffering is my suffering, and their hopes are likewise mine. We are one. In their faces, I see the merciful face of God. How could I stay away? At Lampedusa, Pope Francis addressed so many of the compassion themes we have been trying to unpack. A piece of his homily from the Eucharist he celebrated at Lampedusa will need to suffice.

> Immigrants dying at sea, in boats which were vehicles of hope and became vehicles of death. That is how the headlines put it. When I first heard of this tragedy a few weeks ago, and realized that it happens all too frequently, it has constantly come back to me like a painful thorn in my heart. So I felt that I had to come here today, to pray and to offer a sign of my closeness, but also to challenge our consciences lest this tragedy be repeated. Please, let it not be repeated!
>
> "Adam, where are you?" This is the first question which God asks man after his sin. "Adam, where are you?" Adam lost his bearings, his place in creation, because he thought he could be powerful, able to control everything, to be God. Harmony was lost; the human erred, and this error occurs over and over again also in relationships with others. "The other" is no longer a brother or sister to be loved, but simply someone who disturbs my life and my comfort. . . . How many of us, myself included, have lost our bearings; we are no

longer attentive to the world in which we live; we don't
care; we don't protect what God created for everyone,
and we end up unable even to care for one another!
And when humanity as a whole loses its bearings, it
results in tragedies like the one we have witnessed.

In Spanish literature we have a comedy of Lope de
Vega which tells how the people of the town of Fuente
Ovejuna kill their governor because he is a tyrant. They
do it in such a way that no one knows who the actual
killer is. So when the royal judge asks: "Who killed
the governor?" they all reply: "Fuente Ovejuna, sir."
Everybody and nobody! Today too, the question has
to be asked: Who is responsible for the blood of these
brothers and sisters of ours? Nobody! That is our answer: It isn't me; I don't have anything to do with it; it
must be someone else, but certainly not me. Yet God is
asking each of us: "Where is the blood of your brother
which cries out to me?" Today no one in our world
feels responsible; we have lost a sense of responsibility
for our brothers and sisters. . . . The culture of comfort,
which makes us think only of ourselves, makes us in-
sensitive to the cries of other people, makes us live in
soap bubbles which, however lovely, are insubstantial;
they offer a fleeting and empty illusion which results
in indifference to others; indeed, it even leads to the
globalization of indifference. In this globalized world,
we have fallen into globalized indifference. We have
become used to the suffering of others: it doesn't affect
me; it doesn't concern me; it's none of my business![9]

To regain our bearings, to overcome this globalized indifference, we need to remember who we are and where we are.
We need to hold on to the compassion connection which
realizes that the others are in me as I am in them. When their

---

[9]Pope Francis, "Arena" sports camp, Salina Quarter (July 8, 2013).

world falls apart, we are all broken. We must stay at our posts, taking care of each other; refusing to be lulled into forgetting who we are by a culture of comfort and privilege while others are deprived of what they need to survive.

A Shift in Perception:
The Eucharistic Meal Makes Us One

A friend of mine returns to her home on the Mediterranean coast of Italy each summer from her seminary post here in the United States. She loves her time at home and has often referred to her experience of relaxing by the shores of the Mediterranean as her encounter with "Blue Heaven." But Francesca returned from Italy this past summer with another awakening, which has touched her deeply. She had been reading and reflecting on the thousands of men, women, and children who drowned that past year in those same waters of the Mediterranean, as they sought refuge from war-torn Libya. Suddenly, those waters became for her a "Blue Cemetery." I listened attentively as Francesca shared her ongoing reflection on that tragic spot where so many had died. She began to think that those waters provided the fish that she and her family ate and lived by. The bodies that lay in the sea were now in the fish and the fish were in her. The lost refugee people were in her. In her body, death gave way to life. Eucharist is shared in that mutual gift exchange which now empowers and compels Francesca to live and work for the sake of those refugees who never found the better life they sought. She must be with and for so many other migrating people for their sake. For they live in her, just as God lives in her, physically as well as spiritually.

Threatened by a Pull to Disconnect

We live in perilous times here in the United States, not because we are threatened by the same destructive economic, social, religious, or political injustices that force millions to flee their homelands. Our great peril takes the form of so many alternative messages and images that crowd out the deeper word and larger vision, which sees all people as our sisters and brothers for whom we are here to care. Many will remind us with good reason that the image of the Twin Towers of the World Trade Center crashing to the ground and killing three thousand on that beautiful, sunny morning of September 11, 2001, awakened us as a country to our first responsibility. We must protect ourselves from all those terrorists who are out to get us. The numbers and various motives of those terrorist groups have grown in the years since that horrific event shook our nation. But those who resemble Middle Eastern people continue to pose for many of us the greatest threat. In an attempt to protect ourselves from that very small group of people who would do us harm, we are tempted to close our eyes, our hearts, our country to all of "them," just to be safe. But will that make us safer, better, securer? Once again, the complexity of issues around protecting our borders is real; it is beyond my competence and my goal to analyze them here. But I do believe that in listening to the stories of migrant and refugee people who have come to live among us, we have much to learn, much more than we have to fear.

Stories That Can Save Us

Just the other day, a friend of mine was sharing about a refugee family from the Congo who has moved into the parish she serves in Glyndon, Maryland. When Cealy spoke about what it has meant to her parishioners to have Frank and his family with them, she acknowledged first of all the value of putting real names, faces, and personal stories on this anonymous group called refugees. Each refugee and migrant is a real person with the same hopes and dreams we share. But in addition to the gift of each personal encounter, from which

Frank's new neighbors benefit, he unknowingly teaches his middle-class hosts so much about forgiveness, trust, and gratitude, Cealy explained. The lessons come from the family's witness even more than their words. With so many reasons to be bitter and vengeful toward the Congolese paramilitaries and rebels who had harmed them and destroyed their lives, there is only talk of their shared, but wounded humanity. All of them have suffered, victims and oppressors alike, and forgiveness is the only answer to their country's and their own personal healing. Of this, Frank is certain. "He radiates peace," Cealy mused in her own pondering:

> and in his presence everyone feels welcome. It's such a paradox! We think of ourselves as the host and this family as our guests. Yet in their openness and vulnerability, we feel so valued and trusted. In their presence, I sense that we, too, are more open to trusting one another. They are such a gift for us, who normally are so cautious and self-protective; we tend to keep our worries and insecurities to ourselves. But Frank has shown us that, after losing all, he still has everything he needs. Of what should we be afraid? Suddenly the scriptures take flesh. When Frank first arrived at the parish office, all he hoped for was a good religious education program for his children. And here we, the teachers, find ourselves privileged to become his students. Frank is continuously expressing his great thanks for all his family is receiving here among us. Gratitude for life and each new beginning oozes from him, his wife, and children.[10]

Forgiveness, trust, and gratitude: core virtues for all of us to live by, as we grow into clearer and clearer reflections of

---

[10]Cecilia Cyford, SSJ, reflection offered on Saturday, April 8, 2017, Sugar Loaf Conference Center, Chestnut Hill College, Philadelphia, PA.

the God of compassion whose image we bear. One refugee family meets one middle-class American church and neighborhood, and almost instantaneously fears of "the other" are replaced by the mutual gifts exchanged. The compassion connection opens all of us to become larger versions of ourselves, making room for others in our decluttered *rechem* hearts.

Father Dan Groody from Notre Dame is both a scholar and practitioner whose work and life are dedicated to our contemporary migration challenge.[11] Recently he spoke about the power of this migration experience to save our church. In its ongoing need for reform and change of heart, its dynamic communion pull downward to grow smaller, poorer, and more humble, our church has so much to learn from those who seek shelter and solace, as refugees, among us. Pope Francis is leading the way, but he cannot do it alone. This pilgrim people that we are must ever be on the move toward the homeland God prepares for us, where trust is without borders and compassion is a circle excluding no one. Until that great and glorious day, when we will be One People, beloved and divine, we are all migrating people. In the face of one refugee, we see ourselves, willing to give up all to reach a home where all belong. In the meantime, while on the journey, we have but one responsibility—to take care of each other. This is the cry that echoes from the *rechem* heart of our faithful and relentlessly loving God.

---

[11]Daniel Groody, CSC, University of Notre Dame, director of the Center for Latino Studies and Culture. Dan has published widely on issues and experiences of migration. He has worked around the world from the Vatican to our US Congress to shape policies and influence hearts. I recommend viewing his internationally acclaimed films as well as reading his books and articles. A few books include *Globalization, Spirituality and Justice: Navigating the Path to Peace,* rev. ed. (Maryknoll, NY: Orbis Books, 2015) and *Border of Death, Valley of Life: An Immigrant Journey of Heart and Spirit* (Lanham, MD: Rowman and Littlefield, 2002). Among his films are *One Border, One Body: Immigration and the Eucharist*; and *Dying to Live: A Migrant's Journey.*

That Contemplation May Lead to Compassion: Reclaim God's Loving Gaze

Before this little book ends, a tug from somewhere inside me urges this final invitation: Return to that contemplative place where God's gaze of love makes its strongest claim on you. You may want to have before you a photo or news clipping of a migrant family or child and join me in this compassion prayer. Let God's voice and image rise up in you, as you behold the God who wears this face and utters this cry:

Quiet my heart in this moment, O God of peace, that in Your stillness I may hear this voice of a suffering refugee pleading for compassion. Help me to learn his name and his story; to welcome him into my life. Through Your eyes, may I behold this face of a courageous migrant mother, helping her children cross a dangerous border in hopes of finding her husband, their father. May I do all that I can, may I do something, to make it possible for them to find open hearts rather than closed doors—to be reunited as a family. For, indeed, I believe that they are YOU, YOU—Everywhere, Always—YOU!

This is *kairos* time.[12] As we move from contemplation to compassion, the critical moment of choice awaits us. How we respond to the migration challenge may well determine not only the future of those who flee, but the very identity of the rest of us in their human family, on whom they depend for recognition and a home. Are they our sisters and brothers, bound to us by a compassion connection stronger than any wall, dividing line, or illusion of otherness that we

---

[12]*Kairos* is a word from ancient Greece that means "the right moment to take action."

might selfishly construct? Perhaps, it is the refugee waiting to be met by us, who will dig God out in us, freeing God and us to help save this blessed but broken world that God so loves. Perhaps, what our world most needs is who we have been all along.

Conversation Starters

1. *"We are here to take care of each other." How has the idea of "a compassion connection" expanded the scope of your loving, those you are called to take care of?*
2. *This chapter focuses on the migration crisis as one that affects our entire human family today. How have you experienced "the stranger at your door," either directly or indirectly? Is there a line or story that stirs you to ask questions about your relationship with, or responsibility for, people fleeing their unsafe homelands?*
3. *Robert Schreiter has developed categories for how we construct "the other" as different and separate from us. Return to those outlined in this chapter and consider how you have seen this construction in your own or others' behavior, not as judgment but as a lesson to learn.*
4. *As you sum up this final chapter and the book, what does it mean to suggest that the world urgently needs us to be who we already are—gifts of outpoured love for others, no exception?*